EDITOR-IN-CHIEF
Eileen Cleary

ASSISTANT EDITOR
Elizabeth Mercurio

ASSOCIATE EDITOR
Christine Jones

FLASH FICTION EDITORS
Mark Jednaszewski   Sarah Walker

ART EDITOR
Lisa Sullivan

VISPO EDITOR
Suzanne Mercury

WEB EDITOR
Rebecca Connors

MEDIA AND EVENTS
Frances Donovan

READERS
Susan Kay Anderson, , Jules Jacob,
K. T. Landon. Michelle Lynch, Gloria Monaghan, Catherine Morocco,
Tzynya Pinchback, Huma Sheik Sarah Dickenson Snyder,
Mark Walsh, Anastasia Vassos, Art Zilleruelo

COVER ART, ISSUE 9
Cal Wenby, *Phase*

CONTENTS

YUAN CHANGMING

Lesson One in Word Formations: a X-Cultural Poem

1/ Feminism vs Patriarchy

In Chinese, 妇人(woman) is a girl who's overthrown
A mountain, & 夫人(madam) refers to a human that's
Broken open the sky
While in English
Woman implies her as the wo of man, & *madam* is
Nobody but an other representation of male or adam

2/ Getting Along towards the Same End

In Chinese, 朋友, 恋人, & 爱人 are all
12-stroked characters, just as their counter-
Parts *friend, couple* & *spouse* are 6-lettered
Words in the imperial vocabulary of English

Though they are all underlined with human

Love and loyalty, the former entails twice
As much input or effort of the heart
As the latter to maintain a disparately
Similar humane relationship as a speech act

TOWANA WRIGHT

WE ARE WATCHING

HANGING IN THERE

I AM GREAT

SUZANNE EDISON

That Time the Woman Known as Mother, Disappeared

In the pine tree of my youth

       suckered in sap

           I sequestered myself

       straddling branches   whose scales

needled my skin.

***

Alone   with chickadees   finches   the berating

        squirrels   I sat above

            the forgotten hammock

                        weathering

its knotted ends   like my insides

        while my mother

            draped in white

lay cloistered   in a hospital bed

        room I was not

               allowed to visit.

***

Hunkered on a limb   the air wreathed me

pungent with dandelions   a glister

I used to crush   in sweaty palms   hurrying home

      to make her   a crown.

                    ***

I stayed in that tree

      imagining her   emptied

a devoured pinecone

      and wondered   what could remove

the pitch

               the tarry resin

of her siphoning depression

          the one I had   to avoid.

BRIAN WHITMORE **NIGHT IS DARK WHILE DAY IS LIGHT**

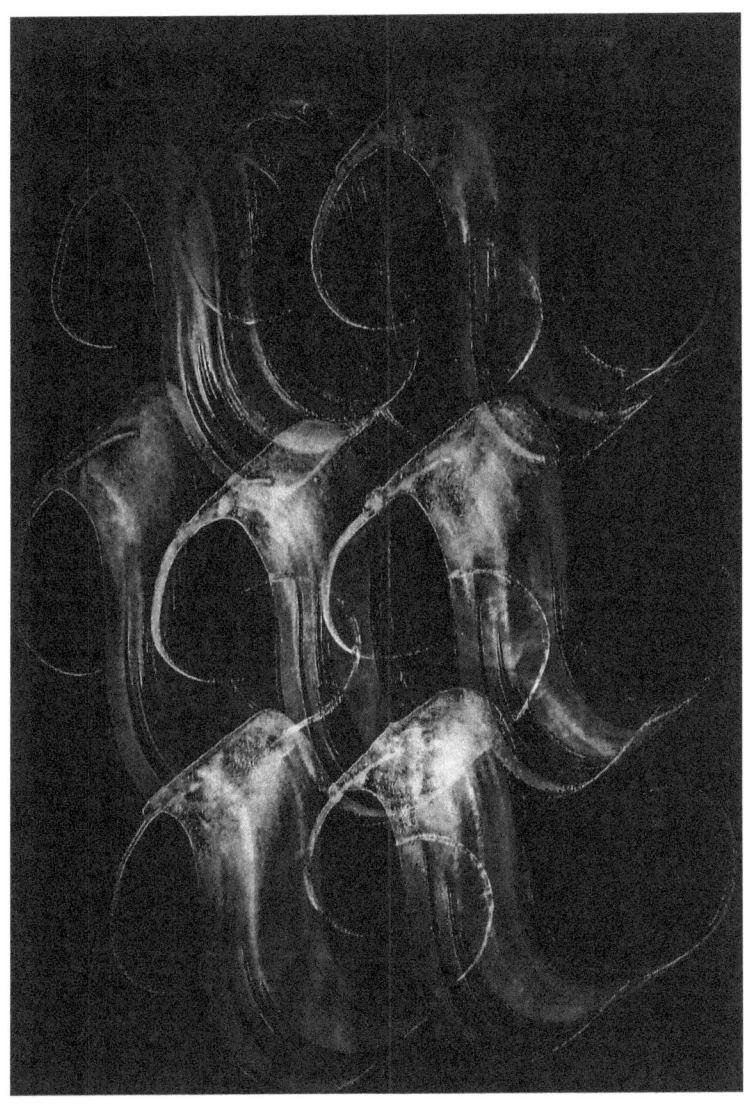

BRIAN WHITMORE   **THE BEGINNING**

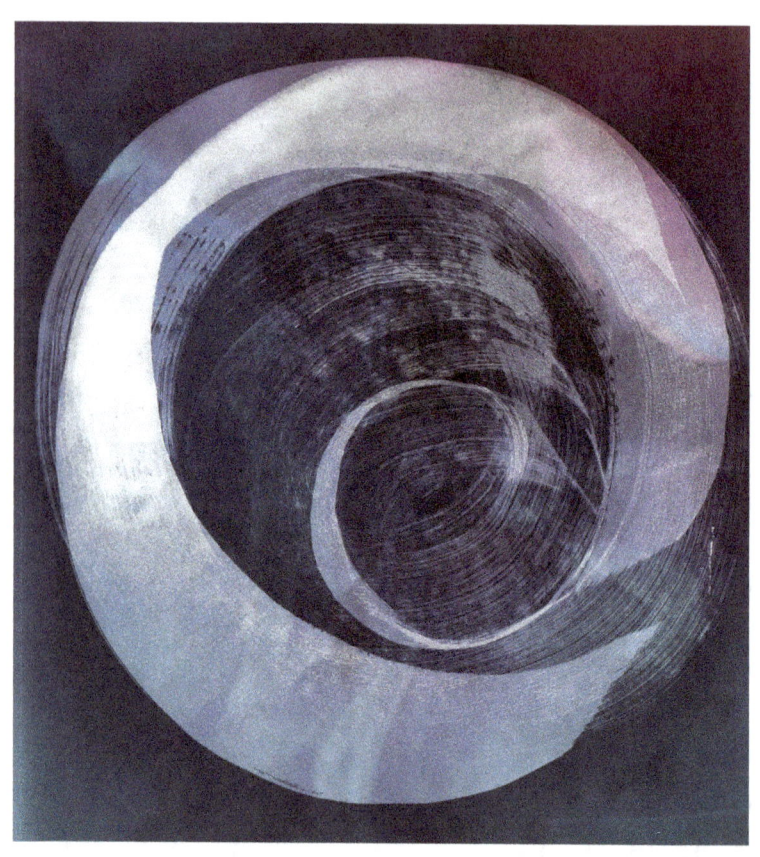

TERESA WILLIAMS

Elegy for W.S. Merwin

Only the gold-ochre notes of the song birds
pierce the morning's semi-darkness,
while I read the last words
of your poem, "Black Cherries"

and now, a long silence—
        so long I wonder if they will return.

If I had not stopped
in the prolonged light of your late May,
I would never have heard
the mineral colors from those birds,
or the sun cracking red,
or felt this sad happiness
passing through.

I would never have looked out to the world—
Remember this

PAUL ILECHKO

For Lucille Clifton

There were others   lost in the blazing city
unable now to look at her   how many centuries
had this been going on   their lives interrupted
but she still waited   she who was never to be
called anonymous   not once her thirtieth year
was shattered into the seconds that composed it

and there was still the light   breaking through
to where she waited   reflected by the mirror she
used as part of her disguise   watching as it edged
towards the distant blue of Virginia hills   a memory
of sweetness   a memory of children   a place of
sharpness   that sparked with all that she had lost.

CATHERINE COBB MOROCCO

Scatter Your Ashes *Here?*

—Pulpit Rock, Monhegan Island

Under your boots, lichen paints the granite
crimson—giant coals smoldering. Gulls
wheel and lord over our island planet.

Dimpling seas spin out into air,
fall on these ledges. And you,
where do you think you'll be when

your bone flies from my hand into the air?
Drifting like feathers down steep
cliffs into sea roil? You'll just disappear?

Not into gloomy forests, blistering heat,
bleak promontories rising out of slough.
Purgatory is a joke to you. Speak to me

that you won't return a mad, mewing gull,
unblinking, one of the violent rude.
Survive in this lichen's thousand-year milieu.

Spill from its icy crevices in May like blood.
I'll stand on you, melting, blinded by God.

MARY ANN HONAKER

Beast

I am a beast of the field
and I am the field's fury.
I am a beast of the forest
and I am the forest's shadows.

For a long time I thought
I may be human, but the noose
and the snare and the fence
the fence the fence failed

to contain me. I see you have
a beast on a nice tight leash.
He is in your power for now;
perhaps you will keep him soft

under your fingers a while.
I too let my coat be brushed
to a shine, but the clean clipped
fur was never mine, never mine.

When the forest calls I will
always come loping, lanquid,
unafraid under the moon's bald
eye, when the field shakes

like a river-drenched beast
in her fury, I will come,
out of sight of all things tame,
far from the mown lawns

of men's making. I am
the danger of a bear's swipe
and her loosed jaws when
the cubs are frightened,

frightened, when the sun
forgets her cycle and consumes
the roses on their stems,
when the bees faint and fruit

never wakes from the flower,
when the poisoned dead
carpet the forest's pleasant path,
then my rage will awaken.

PATRICIA HANAHOE-DOSCH

Because Sorrow

can't consume the whole
day, though it tries--it really tries--
today there are fresh cucumbers and
tomatoes I picked from the garden
you planted. I make a Greek peasant
salad, slice and chop a block
of feta, slowly. The smell is both
brine-awful and sweet. There

is a cantaloupe from a farmstand.
A woman promised me all had been
picked that morning, showed me
fresh peaches and fresh blackberries,
encouraging me to buy more,

but they were too much
sweetness, too much
for a world gone so dark.

I long for winter, to revel
in the sharp pain of shoveling
snow, of frost on my fingers
when I touch ice hanging like knives
from a roof gutter.

Sorrow lives longer in clouds
of cold fog from my breath
as I walk in the early dark
of late winter afternoons.

Yet, today
I succumb
to sweet, fresh delight
of salad, of cheese, and
sunlight
in each forkful of orange melon.

MARYBETH RUA-LARSEN

Supermoon

Leaving the hospital
I come face to face
with fire and ice.
Only the moon
could manage it,
a canary singing
in this December snow,
setting the sky aflame
while my breath
fogs the windshield.
And weren't we like this?
Opposites in everything –
you house proud, never
a sticky spot
on the kitchen floor,
and me with piles
everywhere
and cat-scratched
furniture.
I know
you weren't ready
to leave,
and this moon
you now inhabit –
burning, burning,
our house
on fire– is close enough
that I can almost
touch
your face.

KAREN FRIEDLAND

Small Tiara

That moment,
in wintertime
when dogs breathe heavily
under blankets,

when the music ends,
and there is silence,
and the neighbor's Christmas lights
blink time
into the night.

This moment
is a low-lit jewel
set in a small tiara
to wear on those special occasions

you may forget
to just draw breath,
to say "oh no, not yet"
to death.

KAREN FRIEDLAND

Easter Sunday

How healing
are the chartreuse leaves
and pure white blossoms
riding a stiff April wind
outside my window,

are my animals
breathing heavily in their sleep
at the foot of the bed

calming me as I resurrect
from a four-hour surgery
that stripped me of lady parts
and cancerous tumors
in so many odd places—
the rectum, the diaphragm!

How miraculous was my young surgeon,
training for years to do his level best
to keep middle-aged women alive.

Spring,
I salute you!
Life, World,
you too.

EVE GLASERGREEN

The Last Archeologist

Burials, out of fashion, and trash,
a vocabulary word for children
on their tour of the landfills.

We've excavated each thing
from the ground: the leggings
with phone-shaped pockets—

I suppose it was soothing to press
connection against the thigh.

We unearthed the petite porn;
tiny women zipped into disc drives
for comfort and fetish.

They burned lifetimes
sorting, mounding, compressing
their stuff.
How Jurassic that time was, seedy
when seeds were planted in trash.

Each of their graves upturned,
to make new room, coughed metal—
steel screws in metatarsals, before cured bones.
We don't leave a mark anymore; no
budding Archeologist digging in the schoolyard.

SHERRIE LOVLER   **THE HEART REMEBERS**

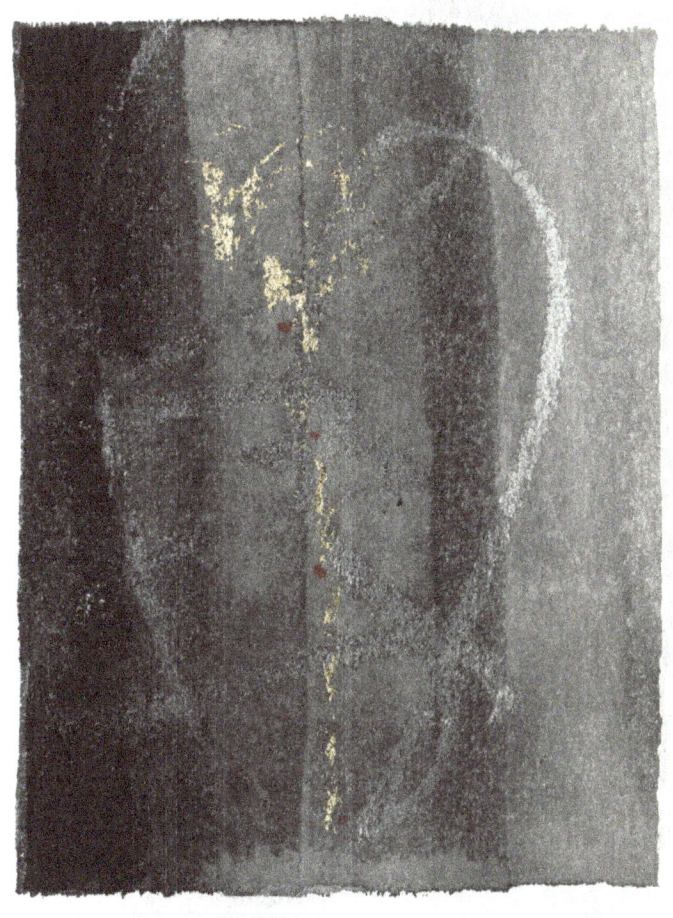

SARA RIES DZIEKONSKI

Closing the Diner

I've married all the ketchups
and Wendell, a widower, is still struggling
to put the zipper pull on track
of his faded blue spring jacket.

His hairs are shoveled piles of snow
on opposite ends of a small backyard.
Beneath the thick ice of his wire frames
his blue ponds show no ripples.

It's warm out, Wendell, I tell him.
You probably won't need that jacket.
I wish he would leave it
two wings flapping in the wind

or drape the sad bundle of denim
over a forearm, toss it in the passenger seat.
He maneuvers the tab again and again
until a certain door swings open

so the slider glides to the old man's chin.
Thank you, he says, patting his pocket for keys.
Wendell turns to me and says
I never get mad at anything.

GRADY DEROSA

Rice Street

he wheels in a mountain
of wet bologna sandwiches

i ask him
is that caviar

and we share a smile
behind a thousand locked doors.

CHAD WEEDEN

Weather Reports

You're in a diner in the middle of nowhere
you've never been, nude as the night,

pouring sugar into coffee because you hate
the taste of metal. You sit at the counter,

unroll silver, push the spoon to the side
like the one you love. The TV's on. Tornado

sirens, and the man caught in the spitting
rain is not impressed by your regrets.

Could have or should have but didn't and won't.
He drags his finger across time

and frames everyone to look like someone else.
But you know better than the camera's blur, the way

he spins around and breathes into the microphone—
I thought the sky only collapsed in rearview mirrors.

You have to retrace your geography for a storm
worth believing. And soon it's egg shells

on blistered linoleum. A peninsula of abandoned cars.
We all think it's a test but it's not. The waitress

clicks her pen. Stampede amnesia. You didn't order
an omelet with toast, but you eat it anyway.

Jägerbomb

A bomb is still a bomb even if it's
made at a bar. Shots are lined up
even with the eager drinkers—all
singles looking for a night, one-
on-one, to consume a new menu, a
new tongue. With enough explosions/
heat-seeking missiles, you'll do

ADAM DAY

Separated from Plimpth

Bright tenants,
horned toenails,

late with late-rent-
fee; the children

of their parents.
The warehouse

floor flecked
with skeletal stretches

of pollen like salt
veins. Time-stained.

Statespeople
babble crawling

the bog, babble on,
mouths full

of wet leaves.
Human furniture.

CHLOE YELENA MILLER

After I Die, Remember All Of Me

This glass jar? I love its
ample, rounded bottom,
and small glass handles,
not big enough to hold onto and lift.

I fill the jar with beans, grains, chocolate chips,
sometimes coconut flakes. Whatever remains
and needs a container.

On one side, the surface is marred
with glue. I tried to soak, freeze, peel, wash, scrape
off the label, but these ridges of glue remain.

No matter the imperfections,
despite or because of me,
I fill the jar again.

CHLOE YELENA MILLER

The Bed Lost Its Lives

Study abroad middle-management,
I reported a list of broken things to
M. in maintenance.

My Italian was rusty or
just not great.
When screws fell out of one bedframe,
I reported it.

The bed lost its lives,
I wrote in Italian,
replacing the word for screws with lives:
vite instead of *viti.*

We had a laugh
and he fixed the beds

but here I am, twenty years later,
remembering the lifeless bed

and all that can go wrong
without the right words.

CHLOE YELENA MILLER

But the Woman?

Images of overgrown babies trying to crawl
out of bellies like chicks out of eggs.
The babies fight against their captors,
inside-out mothers.

But the woman?

She's faceless in these images held high
at protests. She's not given a voice,
not shown fighting for herself.
Her mind, her past, her choices, all absent.
The diary she wrote in, listed places to visit one day,
the ones with rivers and history,
missing.

I let her speak, make her own choices.

JENNY GRASSL

Pastimes of the Sane: ClaytonChooses a Prime Time Bride.

I don't hate Clayton   bachelor unmoved   not breaken
            in oakum skein of harem hair   gloss waven with starry ices

schools of lakemen and lakemaids breath-dangle suspense in T.V. steam
          studio live blue   swim screen with clotten milk

high in silica   pool superhot like you Clayton   in a north
             prone in pixel glam selfie loss licken   I don't hate Clayton

unmarred   unmarried man   girls baiten by battened down boutonniere
          they wanten and they *outen* all their kiss

what lullaby do you fracken on evening's cradle
        your luxum chasms mothers for your children   I don't hate Clayton

thirty women with eggs   *cries echoing*   would you even read
             the caption   your eyes siphon a god— you as victim

not the strappy gown down   cast damsels   Gabby and Rachel   women you narrowen
        the choice to   Rachel crumples on a stair   *happened*   it is written

about this filmed but real grief   your words   it was a show she croven
        didn't she have a plan for loser   *heavy sigh*   your squirm behoven

where you were born   Eureka   *wrong fucking answer* Gabby scoffs
          spitefully bleepen   *it*   Rachel's moment of profundity spaken

at his love news —*I love you both*   *but her more*   I don't hate Clayton
      Susie is The One—fled brood hen clucken not yet fucken

40

EDGE OF THE WORLD

BARBARA CANDIOTTI **THRU A MIRROR DARKLY**

MICHAEL T. YOUNG

The Barn

The tall grass to me seems taller, trying now
to remember it after so many years.
Memory tends to stretch things out,
even the valleys of Oley where my cousins
had their farm, and the field where we played
baseball and other family games that rankled.

Joe could knock the ball to the near edge
of infinity, where the house and barn floated.
My dad ran with the grace of a limping ostrich.
My cousins and I, too little for serious play,
could hardly keep the gloves on our hands.

The ball cracked skyward, or driven down
to be lost at our feet, the runner pushing
against the drag of the grass, the drag of
money owed, favors expected, counting
the payments toward balances that never came—
it was all a clumsy sprint through resentments
for the length of a pitch or the dive home.

Home, where we thought we were or could
get to by winning, because we were never taught
how to lose with the elegance of those birds
that were chased into flight as we circled the bases,
everyone holding close their score of who owed them.

I was too young for scorekeeping, but still
I craned to see over the tufts of field grass,
high as a wave rising over my head.
I kept my eyes fixed on the barn roof, its gable
like the hull of a ship drifting in the clouds,
a buoyancy that somehow kept me from drowning.

ELIZABETH LOUDON

Shift

At dawn the house
moved downhill a little -- not far,
but an inch is enough to nudge open
a crack the width of a quill
in zig zags across the kitchen wall.

It's an old house, chipped
tiles behind the wood stove
and a twist of staircase, the last tread a trip
we forget when we're tired,
carrying the lantern or steaming mint
up to the evening room with a view.
A fortune to mend, right down to the sills
which buckled beneath the weight of stone.
Men come and say they can't help,
and in their eyes a naked relief
that they're driving back to the city.

They warned us we lived
in a seismic zone but the earth stayed quiet,
the bees in their meadows and the hay
in the loft. We had cattle to herd,
we knew the price of each head
and the cost of the price,
and only last autumn,
before the weather turned in an hour,
we climbed to the summit together
and ate ripe plums and cheese,
bread that we tore into two,
enough for a day that hung like a quiet bell
between two nights.

ELIZABETH SYLVIA

Allegory of the Cave

There's a jay trapped
in the truck cap
my husband
has set down
on the driveway.

With furious
disbelief he flies
at the cap's
window, again,
again, refusing
to believe its
material presence.

Bang, bang, bang
against the plexi
with his
panicked wings.

He could escape
by hopping out
the way he came.
He'd need to be
more calm
to think of that,

able to see
the world
within the cab,
not just
the garnet fringe
of the maple
outside.

RADHA MARCUM

Four a.m.

I am a kingdom overmastered by nests.
I am crows in a broken cottonwood.

In the aftermath of nothing-in-particular,
I seep. I clench next year's leaves.

I'm certain I have incubated calamities
in a nest lined with ill foliage.

I peck desiccated flies; I gizzard
mortalities the dog sleeps through.

No sun hatches over the plains.
No relief molts the mountain's side.

I pray for snow glitz to shiver it all.
I claw the sheets.

No call roosters me back from this.
The neighbors' ducks sleep in their crates.

NORA PACE

Matchbox

not enough space to measure
the fields I want to walk
the sky I want to bestow upon you
All we have
is this tiny apartment
and the smallness of our hands
small, I mean, by classical sculpture standards
small in that they can't hold much more rainwater
than a cat's mouth can.

LISA J. SULLIVAN, ART EDITOR

Interview with Jeff Oaks

INTERVIEW WITH VISUAL POET, JEFF OAKS

By Lisa J. Sullivan, Art Editor

It is my pleasure to introduce to our readers the visual poet, Jeff Oaks, who teaches writing at the University of Pittsburgh. In this issue of Lily Poetry Review, we feature his striking visual poetry project called "Changes," which was created using the novel of the same name by Danielle Steel.

Q: Jeff, thank you for spending some time with us today. I know you have had two books of poetry published by Lily Poetry Review Press, *Little What* and *The Things*, and your poems and prose have appeared in a variety of literary journals, magazines, and anthologies. Is this your first venture into visual poetry?

A: Hi Lisa, thank you and *Lily Poetry Review* for taking an interest in these pieces. I've long been interested as a reader of erasure poems and things that connect texts and visual work. I loved poets like Kenneth Patchen's visual work when I was young, but I didn't exactly know how to do it. Or maybe I mean I wasn't brave enough to try. Because I have a very visual mind, I've always been attracted to strange combinations of words and images—Eduardo Galeano's little monsters that exist in the margins of his fantastic books; Anne Carson's *Nox*; Maira Kalman's amazing books; Lynda Barry's books like *What It Is*, to name a few. It wasn't really until I saw Sarah J. Sloat's *Hotel Almighty* that I really felt like this was a world I might try as a creator of this kind of work.

Q: In your opinion, how do visual art and poetry intersect? At what point do they become one, as a separate entity?

A: I'm still learning how connections might happen, and every attempt I make, I learn something new. It's not straightforward, which I appreciate because it continuously surprises me what shows up as I work. There are times when the image is an extension of the language, and there are times when it's a kind of antagonist, a kind of resistance to it. One thing I knew I wanted to think about was how to write a poem that wasn't a caption to an image and/or make an image that wasn't simply an illustration of the language. I wanted them both to exist on their own, if possible. The reader is the place where the two things intersect, of course, where the page asks the reader to experience them together. As the first reader of these pieces, what I'm waiting for is the moment when the language and image vibrate together in some way without disappearing or being absorbed into each other. They don't all work to the same degree for me, but that's the ideal. For me, language and image normally feel as if they exist in separate parts of my mind, so the moment when I can experience them at the same time, it physically feels good. And it's a different feeling than getting a poem right or getting a painting to come together.

Q: You mentioned this project was inspired by and/or culled from the romance novel *Changes* by Danielle Steel, and that at the time of creation, you were going through a series of changes yourself. Can you elaborate on that a bit, to whatever point you are comfortable? Did finishing your project "Changes" feel cathartic?

A: Really there were a series of shifts. In 2016, with the election of Trump, I momentarily lost all my faith in words to convey truth. Kind of surprisingly, I started to paint as a response, which was providing me a new outlet and experience of resisting despair. Then at the age of 55, I published my first book of poetry with Lily Poetry Review Press, with another to follow a couple of years later. Both books dealt with issues of my youth and my middle-age, so I was suddenly untethered from a project to occupy me. In 2021, I was diagnosed as a diabetic type 2, which is an issue in my family, and I felt it as a marker that I was reaching a certain point in my life where I'd have to be much more intentional about how I lived, ate, worked. I felt myself thinking about retirement from teaching. Who did I want to be in this last third or quarter of my life? I'm not usually content to just drift along until something bites me; I like inventing projects for myself. But I literally didn't know what I wanted to write about. I felt both empty and overwhelmed by possible directions.

In the past, when I'd reached a crossroads like this, I'd consulted the *I Ching*, whose other name is the *Book of Changes*. It's a wonderful psychological tool to move your thinking forward. You cast the hexagrams while thinking of a question, and the hexagram that's constructed suggests an answer or a set of actions to take or not take. I thought at first I might write a sequence of poems, each titled with the question I was asking then: "How Should I Live Now?" I would write out from the answers the hexagrams offered and see if I couldn't shape them into poems. That turned out to be too daunting or too simple because I never really felt compelled to do it.

Then when I read *Hotel Almighty*, which is a project in which Sarah J. Sloat used a Stephen King novel, *Misery*, as a source text to create really striking work, I thought about using the *I Ching* similarly—to draw into it or paint into it. The problem was, though, that I liked the *I Ching* too much to "destroy" it.

So one day I was out walking the dog, thinking about all of these things, and I walked by a used furniture store that had a bookcase out front with a "Free Books" sign. I looked through the books until I found Danielle Steel's novel *Changes*. I laughed at the weird coincidence. The word "Changes" blazed out from the spine, and I instantly thought "This might be my *Misery*!" I took it home and started cutting pages out of it to work on.

Q: What drew you to the novel *Changes*? Did you read it? Are there parallels between your project and the novel?

A: Its title gave me the connection between the thing I wanted to write about—my own changing life—and the too-sacred text of the *I Ching*. Here was a text I could cut up. It was free. It was simultaneously "trashy" literature and a bestseller for Steel, her "masterpiece" which likely made her a lot of money. That its best days were behind it now evoked in me a kind sense of pity that, of course, I was also probably feeling for myself.

Have I read it? Not really. I read the pages I work on, so I am following the story of a divorced, professional woman with kids who falls in love with a widowed, famous heart surgeon who also has kids whose trauma about their dead mother he has never known how to heal. The president of the U.S. is shot, and the doctor has to save him. And she, because she's a TV journalist, interviews him and falls in love. The president is saved, but then comes their complicated courtship in which their two professions keep them at a distance for a while. They are both, however, so wealthy that they end up having week vacations in Vale or places rich people go. Eventually, I assume, everything works out, although I haven't read that far yet. It's a very conventional plot by literary standards, which I also had some interest in digging into—seeing if I could find interesting poems within such conventional language and structure.

Although I share nearly zero similarities with the characters, I do really live a fairly conventional life—teach full-time, walk dog three times a day, go to the same places, keep a kind of routine other people might find boring. I like it though, because it is boring, and it lets me bore deeply into myself. What I mean to say is that I feel as if I was in danger of being a conventional text myself. This project gave me a way to maybe change that, find something new.

Q:	What media did you use for the visual art part of this project?

A:	List of ingredients:

1.	One abandoned novel, hardback, with good paper and text.

2.	An Exacto knife, a glue stick.

3.	Pencil, a variety of markers, my favorite Kuretake Brush Pen, a variety of watercolor pencils.

4.	Acrylic paints, a variety of smallish brushes.

5.	Some destructive or disruptive energy in your body you'd like to make use of.

Q:	Can you briefly take us through the process you use to create one of these visual poems?

A:	I start with a handful of pages I've cut out of the book. I flip through them looking at the shape of the paragraphs or amount of white space, and most often I find myself caught by a word—"dragon" maybe, or "words" and then draw a box around it/them. Then I scan the page quickly looking for other language—either a word that gets repeated or a set of interesting words I'm interested in seeing how they might be brought into a new relationship. I draw light boxes around those words and see if there's a way of making some sentence structure to connect them vertically or horizontally or more haphazardly that will require me to draw arrows for readers. When I'm pretty sure I've got something, I ink around the boxes. Then I start painting or drawing in shapes around those words. It's something like creating a tree by making the leaves first and then filling in the trunk afterward. Sometimes the shape around the words is abstract—columns of paint, just shapes of color. Sometimes a clearer shape appears to me—a bedroom with a window, a landscape, a vase. About half the time is finding the language, and the other half is creating the image.

Q:	What is the role of color in your visuals poems, and how did you go about choosing the colors? Did the content of your found poems have anything to do with it?

A:	Originally, as I was just practicing these, I used whatever nearly used up tubes of acrylic paints I had, because they were small and easy to carry around in the small box I take with me to cafes, where I mostly work. The tubes were almost always colors I loved: teal, yellow-green, copper, orange, white. I was drawn to painting the pages because of color and texture; two very physical things which bring the painted parts of the page forward. I've loved experimenting with opaque paints which completely hide the other words, and more translucent colors which allow some of the surrounding language behind it to whisper. I've opened up the kinds of color since then, but I still love and probably gravitate around those original colors. I'm especially partial to the copper and gold acrylics which call back to old, illuminated texts to me.

Q: I'm enthralled by the quiet ambiance of these visual poems. I believe it flows from the open space between words and phrases, which allows the readers to pause and breathe as we are led through each piece by your directional black lines. Do you strive to achieve open space or does this happen more organically?

A: It's definitely organic. It's an effect that happened because of the way I was working, moving individual words or phrases through a field of color or shape. Because I love sentences, my more traditional poetry is almost always syntactically organized; the reader starts at the first word on top and moves vertically down the page until the end. I adore that kind of tight, musical organization. What these pieces allowed me to work on was a more disordered or discontinuous syntax—to be more playful in many ways, to be more trusting of the reader and materials too!

Q: About how much time did you spend creating this project, and how did you determine when it was complete?

A: It's definitely not complete. I feel like I'm about midway through. The goal (a kind of arbitrary one) is to have 64 pages that work together in some way like the *I Ching* (which has 64 hexagrams). So my present goal is to keep generating pages until I have a lot more than 64! I think I officially started it in December 2021, when I was making two or three a day sometimes. Then life interrupted, and I stopped. I made more in July and August of 2022, while waiting to find out about how my chemotherapy would be "staged" (another big change there!). Then I did some more intermittently this past fall. I'm not unhappy to have this slightly discontinuous work schedule because when I do get some free time, this project feels like a joy and escape from my otherwise very continuous life. They are not autobiographical as much of my other work is, so I don't actually have a sense of how to complete this.

Q: Are there other visual poets whose work you admire?

A: Beside Sarah J Sloat and Anne Carson and Kenneth Patchen, there are many poets who've been pushing the boats out for visual poetry—Jen Bervin's *Nets* was an important book to see, as were Stevie Smith's poems and drawings (I love her wildness very much). I've been keeping an account on Pinterest of poets and also a number of artists who make gorgeous pages out of texts and lines, paint, and collage. Many of the artists don't really rise to the level of poetry for me—in the sense that the words on the page remain as texture only or often as cliché—but I'm continually in awe of the visual power of their pieces. I'm also interested in what's called asemic art as well as really any mixture of image and text, some of which seems to be a new thing I wouldn't even call poetry, but is something with a dynamism and energy that is all its own.

Q: Do you have any advice for artists/poets who may want to try their hand at visual poetry?

A: In my classes, as a kind of preparation, I give my students a very rich text (usually Xerox pages from Diane Ackerman's *A Natural History of the Senses*), then give them 20 minutes, using only the words in front of them, to write a love poem. After that, using whatever words are left, I ask them to write an elegy. If we have time, I ask them to write one more thing: a curse out of whatever is left. It helps to unmoor our minds from a kind of sacred duty to respect the text.

Then, if you can do that, start with a single page from a source you don't care about. Tear it out of its book if you can. That destruction itself frees all sorts of wild energy! Give yourself 15-20 minutes to use whatever text is in front of you to write a love poem or an elegy, if you want. Draw light pencil boxes around the words you need, then shade in everything else, and see what you have.

Q: Are you working on any new visual poetry projects? If so, when can we expect to see them?

A: I'm working on "Changes" as I get time. It's my only visual/poetry project. I have at present three other things going on: a nearly finished book of prose essays; a half-finished book of poems; and I need to paint about five more paintings in preparation for a show of my paintings in June.

Q.   Thank you, Jeff, for your generous answers and for allowing us to showcase your stunning, intriguing work.

A.   Thank you for your interest! And for helping me articulate this work I've kind of stumbled into.

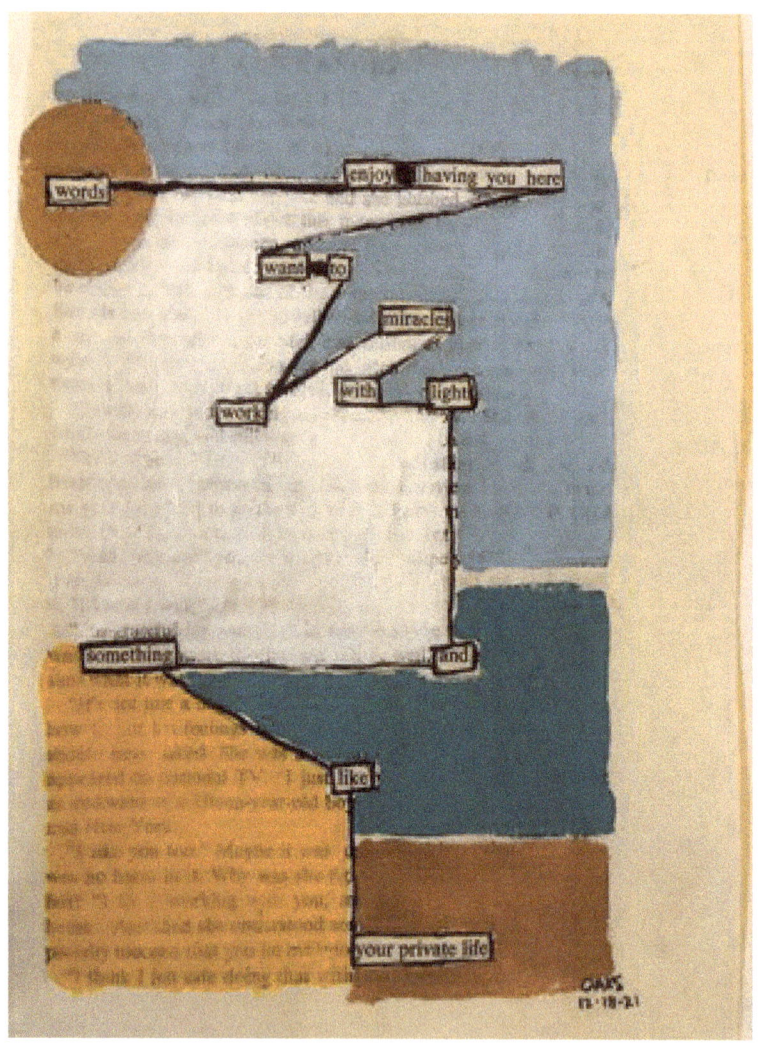

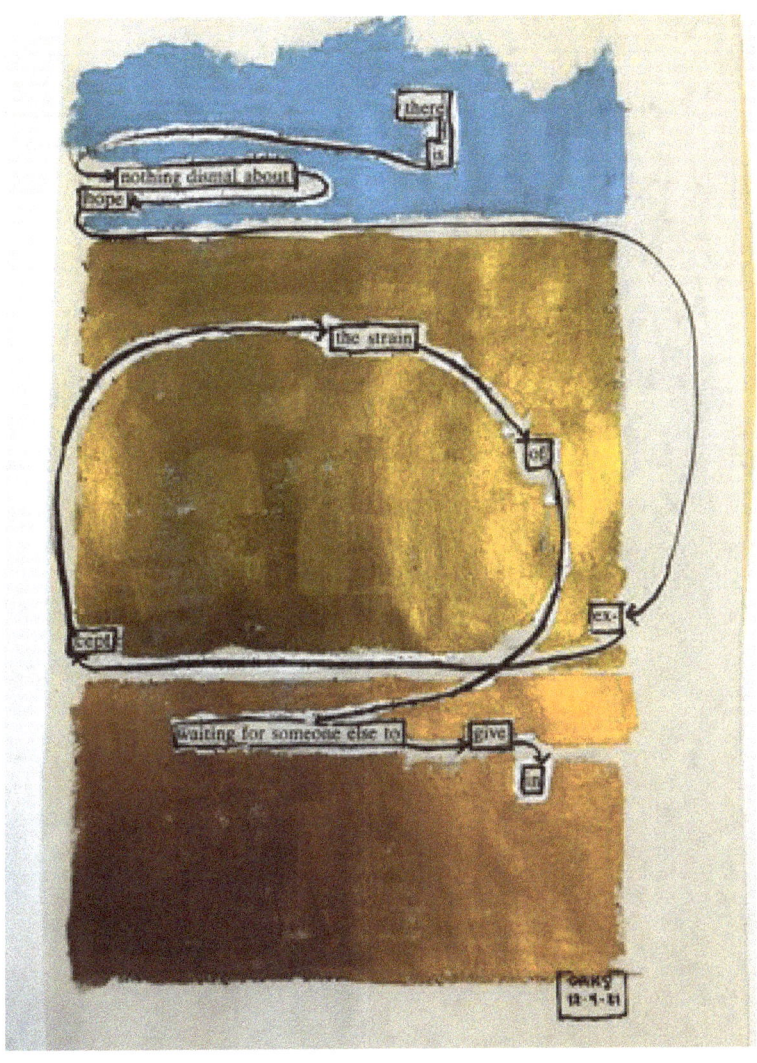

ONE WAVERED

JEFF OAKS
HOW LUCKY SEEING YOU

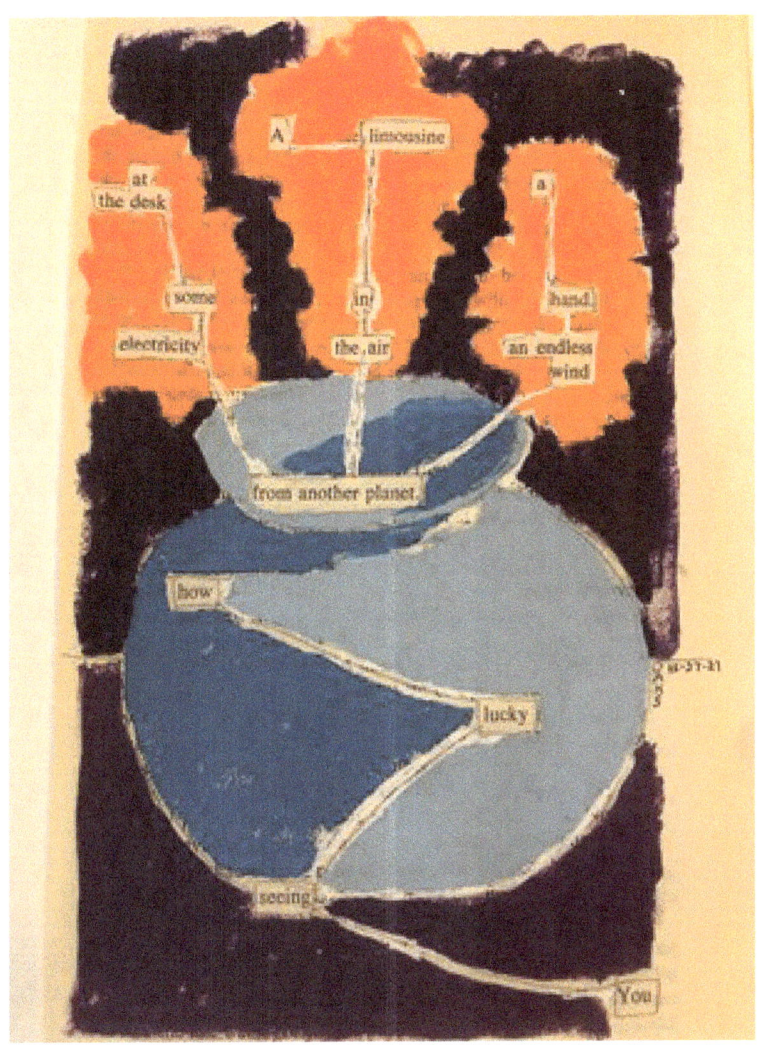

IT WAS NO LONGER

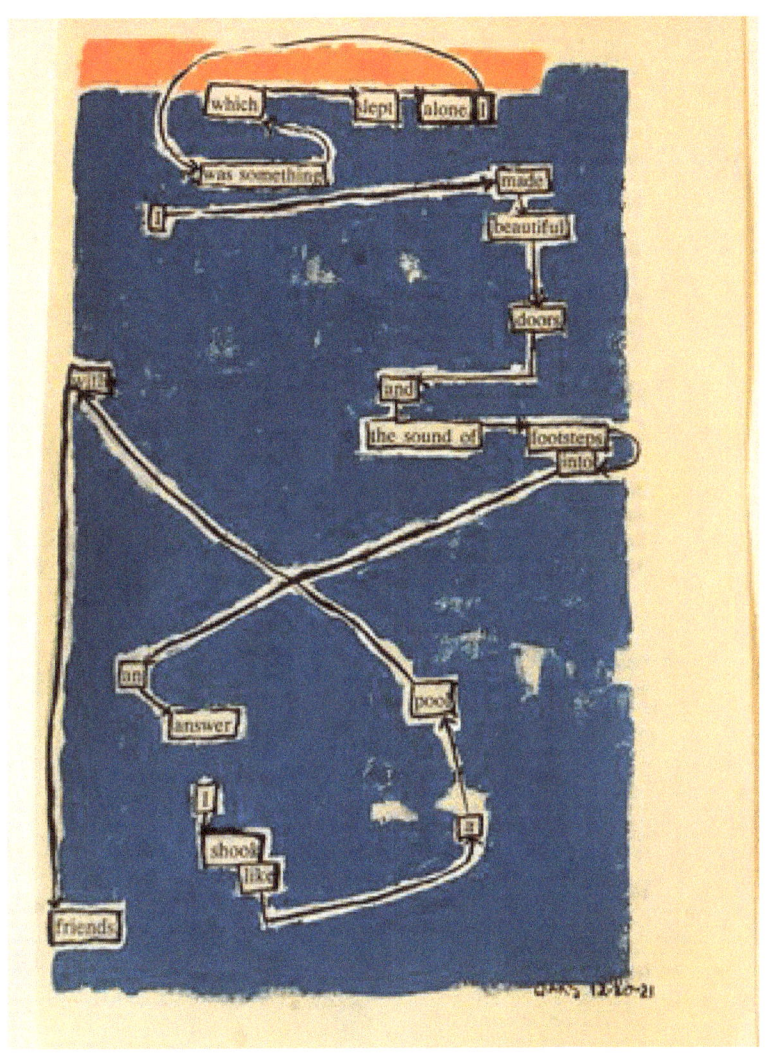

DENNIS DALY

Lilith Appears at the All-Souls Lounge

Shape-shifting Lilith tongues the sea salt
From her lime-clogged margarita.
She's tarried here from the beginning,
Offering those freshly picked apples,
Her garden's best, and neatly drinking
In a storm of built-up reverie.
She observes us with her clan's hunger,
Luring men in with her pellucid charms,
Nourishing their exotic ruins.

The course of history has moved on,
Left this woman lost to time's ravage,
Alone, but with powers intact,
Still engorged, still illegitimate.
Her fidgets beyond the cosmic walls
Cross deep trenches at the origin.
Through the night she flings animal howls,
Fires the star-scape, the launched universe.
But first she comes to this bar to brood,
Bruit gossip with her earth-bound mates.

MARCIA KARP

Once Again, Cain

Cain again fingered his face for his fault,
his protection—the taint of his trespass and blessing.
For nobody marked him. Nobody knew
who he was. He'd thought they would. He wished
they would—bereft and alone, unrelated.

·

His father had favored his brother—the fat
and the first of the flock put to shame tendered fruit.
But he'd been the firstling his father had fathered.
He'd grown to love gardens because of his parents –
luxurious stories of love, fruit, and labors
of love were his fables. He'd learned all their lessons
and those the wind whispered to warn him – the least son
(he thought) – of something desire once did.
His gift was good. His father couldn't
speak ill of it.

If Abel had not
fed his flock the fruit disparaged,
despised, despoiled (since father-shunned),
Cain wouldn't have wished him dead. Wouldn't
have wondered if wishes could kill when at once
Abel died. His parents didn't blame him
or know that spilt blood found its tongue
in foul accusation crying *Cain*.

Someone cried murderer, *breaking our mourning.*
(Our service was private – one son and two parents
who thought they were the world. Who'd
dared disturb first grief?) Cain went east

·

to a sleepy little land
of brothers and mothers

62

and fathers and sons
known now to each other
as butchers and bakers and thieves.
Cain called himself a student
and studied well their manner.
He tried his hand at baking.
He tried his hand at thieving.
He tried to live as if he were a man
like any man.

He studied well the way love was.
He thought he wanted love.
He thought he was a kind man.
What seemed like love was loneliness cut back,
which flourished when she left him,
which blossomed when he left her.
His gifts were not for love, he
grew alone, he grew alone.

When someone called him *Cain*,
he heard *and Abel* echo.
Their parents had called them
Cain and Abel, come quickly.
Abel and Cain, come look at the stars.
They'd bounded together towards awe.

When he visited his parents
(their only son now,
first and last, and least
no more, if ever
(outside himself)
he had been),
he always spoke of Abel,
and Eve and Adam were grateful
to hear their lost son's name.

•

Eve was immobile; movement was measured
(some shadow, embodied, stayed her steps)
in impulse – impossible inches impeded

her wanderings. Still, whither she went, again, Adam
went with her. Walking the garden was work
never finished. (They'd only one fruit tree, one flower
bed now, one rusty patch for the fruits
of the earth.) Cain was their prize crop now, cared for
though absent.

They asked me for nothing and that's what I answered with.
Then I heard Cain *on the wind. West*
to my father I came.

•

Something had happened and Adam was wholly
at war against himself. And not trusting
himself, he scrutinized Cain.

Cain's was the last love Adam would ask for,
for Eve was unable to love now and Adam
knew no one save Cain.

(Not needing sleep to dream,) Eve
awoke to find no one and nothing she knew.
Not Eden, not Adam, not even the fruit
on their tree could she name. She called Adam *Torment.*

Cain fought with his father and knew that his father
cried out in secret. Cain had his own fears.
He was all Adam, all Eve, all that he was,
was born in the garden.

Cain, who lived far from the world of the world,
who'd watched, when he'd watched it, encaved in the shadow
of Cain, now went to the world with his family.
But first he told Adam their flower was frailer than
May-snow astonished furled seedlings.

And Adam,

•

in first grief, let Cain call the world
to pluck Eve from his side.

And Eve, being told, gathered strength and opposed him.
Faultier than a serpent's truth,
my child is your calling. No. No no no, no.
They waited. The world came to gather,
transplant, prop, and sustain her. Far from
their garden. And

                    •

Cain found him,
who'd wandered from breath.

Cain hurled a rock against a rock
to smash the air. *My father.*

Cain didn't wonder if wishes could kill,
anymore. Abel had died on his own.
Still, something stayed Cain
from the life he would live – some sentence imposed
long ago. In his wonted cell Cain knew
his crime was made fresh by the death
of his father. The rigors of his death
condemned the vigor of his son
to spend itself amazed, and fruitless.
(Cain held his parent fast, and faultless.)
(Distant kindred cursed Cain's grief.)

Then Cain must tell Eve
as she lay among strangers.
Mother, he's dead.
By his hand?
Yes,
and Mother,
Yes,
Mother me now.

So Eve knew, but couldn't say how.

The body of Adam was buried in bellies
of beasts denied Eden. Its flesh and its bowels,
its eyes were decayed in the maws of the beasts
Adam (*Cain*) (*Abel*) had named.

And sometimes
straight on the wind came his father to Cain,
his scent or his whisper, his laugh, sigh,
or air of him.
The father of old Cain had loved when a young son.
The first of men in his world.

·

Nor kindness nor kin to Eve now was Cain.
Go. I could kill you – Eve now in her turn
sought his harm. Help me. I'll bite you. Help me.
And his weeping for Abel, his weeping for Adam
were titters in Paradise next to this weeping (it
seemed to him now). Eve began
her song and Cain sang in return so he might
not remember his silence towards Adam.
    Can you lift me up, my dear son.
    Oh no, dear mother, why?
    To carry me round so the people can see.
    It would make the people cry.

    Like a child in my arms, sweet mother,
    I'd bring you round the town
    And old friends then could look again
    For what they knew, when you were you.
    Can you go to hell, my dear son.
    It won't take long to go.

Eve might call for Adam or Abel.
She called most for Cain, her companion, her keeper,
who kept her pieces close together.
He'd say: *If I'd only … Oh mother believe me.*
Cain went out when she cried Comfort me, Cain.

·

Once, long ago, Eve told him the story of Cain.
The child you were, Cain, convicted himself
of being a child, a person, alive.
We meant to acquit you of cumbrous charges
that grew as you grew. But we saw our slip
of a boy propagate opposition
to himself.

       As Eve was speaking
what came back to Cain was his infant guilt –
cunning and craven, his crimes were exempted
by pitying parents from penalty. Or –
    some doubt he'd discharge his debt
    if his payments were few and small
    kept him on trial for his faults,
    for his trials, for his doubt,
    from the first judgement due,
    and forever, it seemed.

·

A woman taunted Eve – Abel-less,
Adam-less, less-than-Eve Eve.
Cain, in a lie, said the taunts were for him.
Even then she knew and said no.

Then they called Cain one day.
Eve was destroyed in a fall,
pushed by the taunter in full knowledge of harm.

Cain had to remind himself,
fresh in the loss of Adam, that his loss
was not the sum of Eve's life.
She called and called for a girl she'd been
a girl once with. Or Adam.
When Eve told Cain she had spoken with Adam,
Cain was resigned. *Tell my father,*
dear mother, I miss him.

When Eve would raise her hand to herself,
Cain was unkind. He went to the strangers
who tended to Eve and asked them
to care, for he thought her unfair, though
Eve was diminished, and he hated her then.

Again and again Cain scratched for its roots,
yet he couldn't follow his mark.
Its tangle of runners defeated him.
He always meant not to, but often did,
discount, not his weight, but the weight the world
held him in. Like that time his father,
he'd thought, had favored his brother.

He kept Eve alive because he was lonely.

They called Cain too late, and he came
to Eve, now empty of air, save the fetid
wind trapped (sickening her son)
when all that Eve was, but flesh, went.

                    •

Cain couldn't conceive again ever
containing the wash and the whip he'd once held
to be life. (Held with pure having,
not naming the hold on him.) He felt now
not nothing, but seldom – remembering
some pleasure, some grief, some puzzle of pride.
He who'd brought Adam and Eve, who'd brought Abel,
a delicate language they'd learned, for they'd loved him,
lived level and lone now.

                    •

Fate again figured Cain's face
that no one might know Cain, save Cain.

KENTON K. YEE

TONIGHT'S KIND OF SKY

The old live for tonight's kind of sky, the kind my po-po would lie under knitting after supper, a meal of Napa cabbage and bok choy my parents raised under tonight's kind of sky. One after another, birds and bats flew past her window. No mosquitoes nor memories of childhood came. The windowpane glinted with blue-yellow freckles. Everything was blue but sunlight. The distant suns shone the yellow-white of spring afternoons that warmed the young on planets too far away for us to imagine. I was lingering, ostensibly there to bid goodnight before going downstairs to do calculus homework and translate a page of The Aeneid for Honors Latin. We watched a shadow flap across her bedspread, its wingspan four times longer than its torso, the silhouette of a fluffy squirrel tail swaying on its beak. Po-po was knitting me an old man's sweater vest to wear long after her life—the vest I'm wearing now. A joint on her left index finger was bent from knitting. We sat listening to the pulse of her needles, the yarn slowly unraveling from its skein, the mist of light from every sun in the universe feeding the half-knitted vest, her squirrel silence singing to me all the love she knew.

PAUL VIERA   **HENDERSONVILLE APPLE TREE**

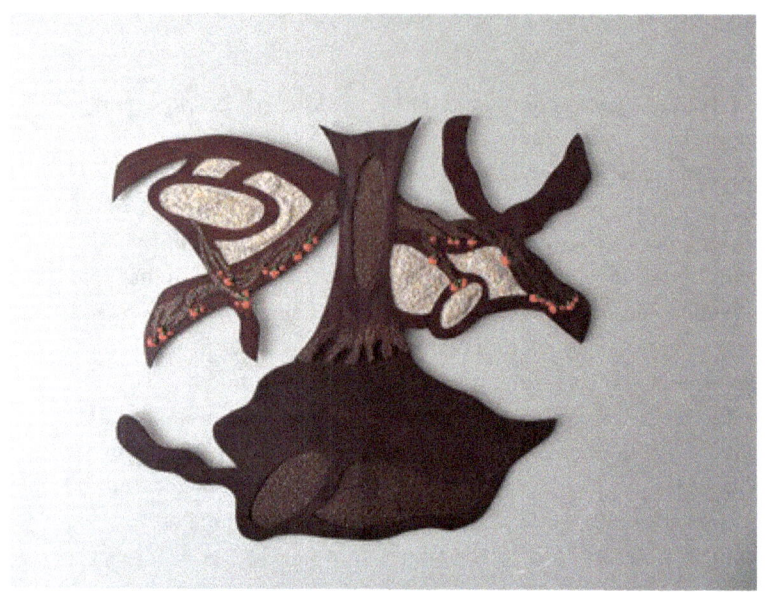

JEAN L. KREILING

Another Four Seasons

1.   Samuel Barber's *Adagio for Strings*

           treading sluggishly
           anguish nudges ash and blood
           stirs winter's embers

2.   W. A. Mozart's String Quintet, K. 614

           wood and string exhale
           a fragrance fresh as April
           song of his last spring

3.   Claude Debussy's *Passepied*

           feet light as giggles
           dance the language of sunshine
           sweet games of summer

4.   Johannes Brahms' Clarinet Quintet, op. 115

           late-blooming roses
           sundials wise as mirrors
           autumn tells the truth

AMY PENCE

Panorama

We travel far – the skies slit open: a seascape, a glacier
a palace for a deposed emperor. Strangers smudge

or stand like nobodies, one-eyed, collapsed, or see-
through. One stands where you thought nothing

had been: eyes look through you to the known
We are exposed, locked and standing in front

of a medieval fortress, the astronomical clock layered
with the zodiac, the 12 apostles turn on the hour. Cuckoo.

Everything that roots us, we left behind. We have local
currency, an ignorant tongue for the language. We

see horizons, turn our bodies to coat the landscape with
our digitals, we digitize it, try to do what a 16th

century painter did with just paint and perspective.
Bruegel, in *Haymaking*, who sees the vista with a god's eye,

captures an outcropping haloed by sky. Above wild fields,
a river, a distant village, a church, centimeter-

tall people ashore. Closer in, hayfields where glyphs
bend with rakes to all that yellow. A triad of figures

trudge off-scene, balancing baskets, one man's backside atop
his horse's. Every person occupied, essential to the scene.

Among three harvesters moving toward fields, there's the one
at the center. Only she sees us, the viewer, like that mysterious

stranger who appears in your panos. She sees you, that elemental
creature, the oddball between two irked women aged

by thankless work. Her round face bears innocence,
a full bliss we capture-- the good of the day, orange

poppies roadside, the vista in concert with the mind.

CAMMY THOMAS

Pestilence

Whiteness is wrapped in the sticky blooms
of mountain laurel, sits with you at the movies.
Polishes your shoes and walks to the mailbox
before dusk to avoid coyotes in the woods
across the street. When the owlet flies on
new wings I watch through whiteness
the creature's pale fluffy face, unblinking yellow
eyes that mark my every move on the path
below tall pines. We tried to suspend
the whiteness for a moment when
our friend died, so we could be totally
there, but we could not let it go.
Where did the whiteness come from?
Not in us, not on us, but around us,
like a mist with no goddess to dispel it.
Wars leave it intact. Violins and ancient
civilizations make it grow. It only
leaves us when—I can't think when.
Whiteness boards the plane
ahead of me. We will keep our distance
from each other and from the whiteness that
bruises its way into everything. When whales
breathe above the surface in slow gargantuan
exhalations, they can sometimes make it go away—
or sometimes planting thyme, but even then
whiteness cloys in the dirt on the edge of my shovel,
veils the little plant I drench. The water cascades
with whiteness. Can there be sorrow when
it's not our place to grieve? Is one death different
from another? The little plant is empaneled
with whiteness, abbreviated by it.
When I lie down, it dreams itself into me.

MARY BUCHINGER

We have left

      the children's table, dear husband
house band - homeland - sole man

its legs kicked out by our sons
hour stuns - flower stones - sorrows shun

let us moo, we are hooves 'n goo
the table, a table of crumble and crumb

MARY BUCHINGER

There is only the sacred and the desecrated

There is only the sacred and the desecrated
                    —*Francis of Assisi*

My cat's expression of holy—
 Me she says bumping my chin
chewing on my pencil

          the rain too is
          air   multiplied

     o

The hardware store our destination
I step off the curb with my dog Dover
on a leash
            the street is empty
the way streets in dreams
are empty   what I see
is what I'm looking for

            the door we'll enter
waits on the other side of the strangely
lacquered pavement—
                    trick of the light
that orangey-yellow-greenish glow
before a storm

            then I spot
the line of metal barricades the reason
no cars
          and a Wolf comes loping
toward us its grey and white coat glossy
in the golden light
            it wants Dover!

Help I say as if to myself *Help*.

          A man looks up
his blond dog peeing on the grass
and I can see he has no idea

              All I can do is wake

          o

Francis what gave you this idea?
 was it the birds their wings of light
and perfect eggs the flesh on the foot
 of a newborn child   the first holy
leaves of anything green   earth's cathedral
 of pumice and lazuli rent-free sanctity
you begin Francis and then you
 begin again a lease on new

          o

The Ukrainian artist was seventy years old
the first time she held a brush
   her husband and daughter buried
   son banished to a penal colony

       I will paint my future she said
              I will give it bird and flower
     blues and yellows   my green
future in a sacred embrace of these walls
 oh concrete surface hold my dream still
and bring it into vine give it window and desk
 let what is me be garden the feathered song
that lives here *Paint it Feed it* and it
 will open in time

          o

Two sisters—
    when one spoke pearls fell from her mouth
       and the other   frogs and toads

   and me Sister Three   (each sister in me)
         in my ears pearls and toads

           amphibious wisdom I
           can take to the road

    o

Bonaventure gave us Francis clean
Francis beloved Who does not need
  an apologist and confessor?
  a translator of our peripatetic intent

someone who sees us
 as their vested interest

        their very lively lovelihood
         (*Be my bon adventure!*)

    o

  say I start right now
paint my house   my inner vessel
with a new teaching—

  a new Francis
 whatever *contuition* is required
to see
    the rivulets of holiness
       in cloudberry and leaf
    in blue spider veins
  and ripening tomato—

to tread the holy path of talking stones
beneath a Sister Moon God's very son a sheep!

     (but Francis   must I empty my freezer
        decouple my household from meat?)

how personal
need an ethic be?

   the exact change

(exact change only)

    o

Dear Frances did you wonder how
the human skin detects temperature?

        your answer is an answer
to everything

    you shed your father's silks
for sackcloth that rasped against your skin
     and gathered in its rough flax weave
       the feathers and fur
      of your new wild friends

   denying self you cured
all you touched   even the water that washed
 your feet came away holy

      water's memory of you
        released the fevers
        of cows

    o

I, branched dowsing rod, seek You
Holiness, to be my find

  O hidden Stream of goodness
call to my diviner, draw on that
in me which rhymes with You

may I sense what I cannot see
persistent and sure as my cat

may we meet as in a state of
before: You coursing under-
ground and me believing

          o

            the refusal
of comfort is comfort

the callous of love can
    not admit bitterness

          o

when I teach about the language
  of intimacy and power

        I teach the words
      that insulate the stark
        request:

    would you mind
  would it be okay with you if—

and I consider the chickadee
the *chick a dee-dee-dee-dee*—
each *dee* a measure of urgency

a thermometer of sound

o

Once in the White Mountains
on the Greeley Pond trail I stopped
by a pine tree near the parking lot
and the chorus of *chick-a-dee-dee-dee*
grew bold and bright one bird
nearest me its throat pulsing with song
called everyone to come   the air flocked
alive   chickadees primed for a handout
and I didn't know this learning they had
and to never go to the ponds without
a handful of seed these birds of Francis
sought Francis in me!

o

Francis, you're the mattress
against the bullet

              Wake up!
The rich are using you

o

what doesn't begin as an irritation?
an unendurable itch— an expulsion
and accommodation   the annoying
undeniable new with no vision of what's
to come
          the Bang begat Elephants and
Sycamores and Shakespeare who knows
what from where

I inhale pearly nights and mornings
and hold the argument in my iridescent sheen
pure making-do I am

o

O grand Machine built to blunder and
bluster
                    feel the inside coil of muscle
and rivering blood
                    listen up Heart you
four-chambered ear
                    hear the little quartet
    of Harmony and beat

        the homogenitor of synching
            pulses raises the ante
        the individual humanoid
        has such thin boundary

        yet   in you little Body
the march of molecules
        the small insistent Spirit breathes
                            its mandate
        the inexorable Animation shared
with all that lives!

        Say to the bristly Jay in the Spruce
bullying its neighbor Squirrel—

        *I-Jay   I-Spruce   I-Squirrel
        I-Keep-of-Flame!*

        (*for now* says the burgeoning eye the swollen
and diseased   the desecrated I)

        o

it was Francis' eyes that did him in
they wept and crusted and pained
him to no end thick-scabbed sick
eyes buckled lids lashes sucked in
and under   scraping his cornea thin
scarring opacity vision turned
inward
   Hello Brother Fire! he said
to the flame recruited to cauterize
the wounds of his eyes

   someone held the fire
     as Francis sang
someone
had to leave the room

     Prayer— his surgeon
  his staff his supper his succor—
till perfectly he saw the six-winged
angel on the cross and welcomed
the gift of the five wounds
calling *Lord my Refuge*
and my Portion in the land
of the living

   o

What astronauts saw they tried out new
language to tell us speech of the almost-died
that beautiful Awful Edge once peered
endears its Pilgrim to its land to its living wild
knowable land   an alcoholic granted a new
liver rarely returns to drink

    the gifts of Extremity

   what in me might be revived?
someone please lend me an eye

o

A child in my dream was full
of judgment. Certain in her
pronouncement   the blue-eyed
girl repeated what she'd heard
evil this and *evil* that poor parrot
ripe for light   (could she be me?)

o

in the everlasting unremitting undertow of expansion
we grows thin
an ache of connection

o

I can tell you how the end happens
says the toad   it's preceded by a
a nor'easter bearing a deluge
wind   rain terrible noise and you
huddle close family neighbors
you feel the dread barely contained
within your clustered shivering bodies
    then the dam gives way and
your home dissolves in the night
morning before you realize truly
the end has come the life
you'd known   impossible

o

The heron stabs a circle of sun
that drips shining droplets and flips—
flash of foil!— then the heron
tilts the sun and
swallows it

whole

      I watch the neck take it in
the disc not fitting   protrudes
from the narrow throat that stretches
up to urge it down to hasten and
accommodate this death
that will give
life

    what's been swallowed
resists the final requirement
does not slip into its conclusion
but grips the walls that confine
bends their frame

            extending its fins
the whole self engages in the search
for its missing sea
its ease of river

            the bird answers
with a beakful of water
then wades through
the reeds

        pausing
to salute the sky

and the disc disappears
from the silhouette of the
heron's neck

    o

each Rose new again
in each season the same
branch the same root
the same plot of soil
offers *Another*
and *Another*

the perfect is a circle
God says this every day

Notes on "There is only the sacred":

Facts about the life of St. Francis of Assisi are taken from an article by Joan Acocella, titled "Rich Man, Poor Man," in *The New Yorker* (2013). Included in that article is a quote from a Marxist critic who called St. Francis a "mattress to the bullet" and said the rich were using the Franciscan Friars. The artist who took up her brush when she was seventy years old is Raika Polina from Ukraine; more information and images of her extraordinary work can be found here: https://naive.in.ua/en/author/raiko-polina/.

MARY BUCHINGER

At the beaver pond

                    what's visible—
their orderly piles

        knitted sticks
    calculation of long-enough
 angle of the gnaw

                        undulating row
      weave of tree – rock – culvert – tree
                slows a stream
                to a
                seep

        and in the distance   a stand of snags
    water-girdled trunks wigged with birds

turtles spill their coinage
on the carpet marsh

    the beauty of this watery path through watery grass—

        what was felt was the guide
            current combing tail and pelt

MARY BUCHINGER

(INLAND)

In INLAND
  (in the _Inn of In_)

   reside the deepest greens
the darkest forest of inside

What's in there? you ask
    again & again

Looking for what?

Neither of us can decide

    still you keep rooting around

         Ø

if not Shore—

      that place
      of meeting

      edge of
  heaving & new

   with stakes of herons
stately in the ebbtide

lively spinning
        of minnow

      the not-rot
  of borderland

  where rushes of marsh

merge
    submerge   pocked

green beds come go
    sucking mud

    o watery depths!—

then

    INLAND
          in amber

(what is*n't* & was*n't* & wo*n't*)

      Ø

threshold foothold toe-
             finger- choke-
                hold

      Ø

Even INLAND
  was once a sea—

    a shallow sea that turned
the living to limestone

        an ankle-deep sea
           of economy

   a shiny miry
      mirror
        of sun

      Ø

But, what's inside? you ask

Which catalog
shall I reach for?
    Living or dead?

There are twisted things—
       chain coral & pincushion & petoskey

   imprints & exprints

there is what was left
when the sun was overhead—

the smallest of shadows
    that grew & grew

   Ø

& there once was a self
 known only to self

who carried the sea
wherever she went—

  skirt of water
  piney shawl

she loved the creatures dead in their shells
she plucked & pickled them
broke & built with them

paneled her house with the dead
white of the shells

   Ø

How are your dead? I ask
  when it's quiet

      & I've forgotten
    where I am

     Ø

  the shoreless interior
    is an airless place
of no coming no going

    a stillborn moon
        vast unknown

incubator
   of storm & misdirection

     Ø

why the brew of strange
  in the End of End
I mean, the _Inn of In_? you ask

      it's awash
    in unabashed selfdom
        & uncontested banshees

    a self-pollinated bloom

   a matter of shrinking
where there's too much room

a skiffless wilderness—

Ø

& here you are
requesting a map
texture you call it

the ups & downs
of topography
the squirrely lines
that tell the relief

in truth

what you seek
are my sinkholes & swamps

the River that runs through me

Ø

Grab your fishing pole
my man!
Let out some line

String your bow
fletch your arrow—

but the wild you seek
is not what lives
in INLAND

(the Prairie long-ago walled
the Sky contrailed)

belt of rust

& belly of stars

Ø

Plato was inside
   & outside of
    INLAND's cave

We know Everything
Everything is known
   remember?

Ø

the skull of the moose
  its white machinery
   of ovals and holes
  emerges from dirt

like a dentist I pick
 at its teeth   test
  their hold
in the mandible

   tap each one
canine   incisor
  rattle their marble

   I imagine a pair of them
in my pocket
  knocking anew

but the clean ivory
     gumdrops
   wedged in bone
 do not yield
  to my hand

the long loop of jaw

signature of its species
        presses soundless
    into the ground

    remnants of horns
spread ear-shaped in air
(the great chandeliers
            missing)

I trace with my finger
    the cup & curve
    of zygomatic arch

    all the meaningful
        spaces here
    are jagged blanks

to look into this moose's eyes
I'd have to enter the earth—
        that other INLAND
        ; the after-birth

            Ø

    A diffusion of light
            catches my eye—

a dead limb
        & live low bushes
    encased in airy aspic

        yellow grasses
                haloed glow!—

    what I see from that side
    disappears from over here

    I approach

looking for what I remember

      & *Ah!*

         a waiting maker
hangs upside down
   inside its tent

      its eyes all eyeing me

I breathe & watch the shuddering
   of the silvery web

      Ø

In INLAND
      you believe
  there's no shore

   that you see
  what there is
& there is no more

the Carnival outside
the unreal that reels beyond

     is an unknowable other
     a deathbed
     a poem

      Ø

the undeveloped film of INLAND
      holds no surprises

   INLAND

everyone is aghast
    I mean, a guest

Can't I live there too? you ask
Not even I do I answer

    its tundra its barrens
      flatlands flatline

      fill & flip
    with windmills
      & ghosts

    Ø

(Plato knew
what the man was looking for
what the woman was missing

    he wrote a myth
    so we'd remember)

    Ø

tillable soil
 striped by
clay-piped
  ditches
browed with brown cattails
    & bruises of lupine

  how I loved the wild
    asparagus
    tiger lilies &
  black-eyed susans
      beside the culvert

  & its tiny salt-less sea
  brimming with snails
   & stone teeth

    Ø

    Burn
what's dead in spring
so greenness
can come in

The new is
always a chore

    Ø

INLAND's a crash landing

 a reedy pond hand-dug
& hand-sewn its catfish
   drowning   its color
      drains   the fabric
thins   its prisons
      abound

all around it is everything
that's real & alive!
     climate
& industry culture &
philosophy every
letter ever sown &
thought that could
be known

  the weight of what
  surrounds it grows

how much can it bear—

Ø

You can drive there, I say
meaning *I* could

I can point my nose
anywhere INLAND & go

Ø

There the cars rise
    from their haunches
  to daily exhaust
    & foul the roads

& the roads themselves
  are arrow-straight stays
in the corset of INLAND

    with its stricture of county
& seat full of judges
        beside the white
    Corinthian columns

(all borrowed
except the geography
& history
    of the used-to-be sea)

Ø

INLAND is everybody
  the same everywhere

  euchre & recipes

Would you bake me a cake? you ask
INLAND I would, I say

I would darn your socks
& cut your hair
we would ferment there

be each other's
well-aged wine—

   It's enough? you venture

No
It's a god-awful bore

Throw off the covers
get out of bed

     (INLAND I am
   wherever we are)

   See, we're almost there!

          Ø

You know we're always talking
about more than one thing, I say

Yeah, I know, you say

          Wait what are they?
     I mean, what's the other one?

          Ø

INLAND we make trinkets
for tourists to buy

they want to show they have visited
they want to believe they've been here

These decoy maneuvers we depend on
    mutual make-believe that each of us is
        who the other says we are

                Ø

Nest algae
        no, Nostalgia

                    the remove
that holds INLAND together don't
try the bonds

don't test
the vision

            but deputize

make every wish
work for you!

                Ø

Inside INLAND
(in the _Inn of In_)
    it's wild

        & desolate
    as the open sea

an unmet shore
of roving grief

            monstrous
       with fossils
and cicadas

            Ø

INLAND is slow & stormy
  undefended   uncountried

    filled with the sadness
       of the unaffiliated

such is the learning
            that happens
      in the absence
of question

the walk of the sleepers
whose feet meet
no tension
       of ground

oh how it echoes

            Ø

But, seriously, what's in there? you ask

You want me to tell you
    a story of INLAND?

It happened one morning
                    at the edge
    of the neighbor's hayfield

    an Eagle leapt from the
                    top of a dying pine
        whipped out wings

the span of a tractor a baler a rake

& swooped down
        to a bed of fawns
    snatching one up
in its yellow talons—

    the Doe bellowed & bawled
drove her hooves into the Eagle's load

 What else could she do?

    the Eagle struggled to rise
with its red & white speckled breakfast

    but the Doe would not relent
she won the body back

& it lay— is there still—
  bleeding
            into the field

EILEEN CLEARY

Book Review: *In the Shape of a Woman*
by **Lily Greenberg** (Broadstone Books. 2022)

The shape appears non distinct at first, a contour of something familiar. You approach the outline of a deer on the side of the road that upon closer inspection turns out to be a shrub. Greenberg writes about the protean ability any of us have to transmutate, even within our given forms.

> My leaf hair caught. In the plumes
> a woman formed and departed.
> I was not her. The lizard
> watched and I said what trees say
> I am no woman.

Sometimes a current form gives notice to the world of what it will become. An acorn becomes an oak. An infant girl might grow into a woman. Though the "thingnesses" of our shapes can never choose what the world labels them, our entities within know and name themselves. Greenberg writes, " my body is a boy/sitting by the window."

This smart, authentic debut explores not only the shape of a woman but the shapes in which women are expected to carve themselves."I'm tired of fasting Jesus, emaciated,/ ribs crowding out this loincloth."

It's impossible to capture this stunning debut on these pages. One must read it and let the "red parade" of its lyrical energy "up end you." But I leave you with Greenberg's assertion that no matter a woman's shape, form, or container, they will not be contained.

> Freedom— I could
> be anything I wanted. Boy
> with a pocketful of daisies,
> Girl outrunning the river.
> Priest of open hands,
> goddess of touch-me-not.

For all of our sakes, I hope that this is the first of many books by Lily Greenberg.

GEORGE KALOGERIS

Book Review: *The Sliding Boat Our Bodies Made* by Jennifer Barber (The Word Works, 2022)

In each of her three superb previous books, Jennifer Barber has established herself as a poet of great delicacy and power, and a master of that most hard-won poetic skill: reticence. But there is also an exhilarating, destabilizing element that lurks in the darkly lit undercurrents of these level-voiced poems, and plain-spoken poignancies can suddenly erupt in genuine epiphany. As with the self-effacing, life-embracing intonations of Adam Zagajewski, Barber's poems are as vulnerable to the predicaments of the world as they are available to the possibilities of rapture.

In the poem "Elegy", Barber concludes with these exquisite lines:

> You *are* the afternoon,
> Nowhere and everywhere.
>
> No one can hear you when you say,
> *Everyone was once summer's child.*

This is the quietest and yet most intensely haunting of echo chambers. Note the immediacy of the stress on "you are" and the inverted off rhyme with "hear you"—internal chimes, spaced far enough apart by the separate couplets to muffle the tolling of loss, even as it perks our lyric ears. "Nowhere" and "everywhere" are rhyming mirror images of absence and presence. And "no one" and the phantasmal "you when" permeate the atmosphere of "afternoon," which then is itself encompassed by the chilling reverberation of "everyone", with its frisson of italics. And here, as we *hear* again just where we *are*, in the very vortex of loss, the visionary is enacted with the lightest possible touch. "If no one can hear you when you say," then it's as if the great phrase, *"Everyone was once summer's child"*, is conveyed as pure sensation. As if the shimmer of the line and the sheer tactile effect of those italics could make the hair on the back of our reader's bent neck stands up—and it does. What more tender example of sublimely suspended transience could there be than *"summer's child"*?

In a harrowing poem of utter helplessness and perfect distillation, Barber intersperses her own lines between quotes from the poetry journal of one of her students, a beloved, deeply troubled young man whose life ended through a drug overdose. Here's the way "In Class" concludes:

A big, gentle, offbeat guy

Diseased skin flakes and falls
My husk peeling like old wallpaper

If we had talked more, one on one

Scraped clean by prying eyes and judging teeth

I collected their journals at semester's end

What a fate it is
To die by one's own negligence

I am nearly transparent by now

For over two decades, Jenny Barber was the Editor-in-Chief of *Salamander*. Her acute skills at honing in and winnowing down, are on full display in the quoted lines. The poet-teacher's notational, cherishing voice, in antiphonal counterpoint to the student-poet's beseeching cry, on the brink of the abyss, is profoundly affecting. Their voices crisscross, from a distance, but not at cross-purposes. Barber's anguished self-scrutiny: "if we had talked more, one on one" and the undergrad's desperate: "*to die by one's own negligence*" hold the fateful scales, for a moment, in quivering counterbalance. A moment no longer than counting from "one on one" to "*one's own.*" The line ending with "semester's end" leads into the one beginning with "*What a fate*". In the aftermath of what the undergrad's verse so accurately foreshadowed, the heartbreakingly accurate, profoundly unemphatic recollection of a self that cannot collect itself: "I collected their journals at semester's end." In a voice as self-possessed as Barber's, and as immune to self-aggrandizement, the last words are the student's, free falling in extremis:

I am nearly transparent by now. I am reminded of Wislawa Szymborska's poem on a photograph of the poor souls jumping out of the burning towers on 9/11. It ends:

> I can do only two things for them—
> describe this flight
> and not add a last line.

In a lovely poem about her daughter, Barber remembers the child's initial attempts at writing: "the marks you made, so dark / they dented the paper's weave." *Why think of it now?* asks the poet, seeing the grownup young woman on her way to her boyfriend's apartment. The memory leaps to a further back assertion of self, back to the child learning to walk, by first standing on her own two feet. "You stood at the center of the world, / in your overalls and round white shoes." This couplet encapsulates the trajectory of the child's growth and the life of the mother's poem—adorable and adoring, their worlds intersect, as the "round white shoes" imprint the page of the poem with the black felicitous weave of the magical letters.

The epigraph to the book is by W.G. Sebald, and the very first poem ends with a distinctly Sebaldian note: "No one's being watched / though watchfulness remains." The fullness of that watching, as though we are in the presence of the ever-vigilant, interrogative speechlessness of the dead, haunts Barber's poems of Jewish history. As a tourist in Jerusalem, "so many prayers are wedged / in the city's throat, / it's impossible to pull them out." In "Orders Concerning the Jews," a litany of restrictions from the Court of Toledo in 1412 ends with "Thus it will be clear / at a glance who they are." The yellow star is not mentioned, but it was already there, a sign of those medieval times. There in that stare. And there in the Holy Land, where watchfulness remains with a palpable trace of Sebaldian paranoia: "A hundred times a day I touch / the passport in my pocketbook / to make sure my hand's still there." In a poem that's set in the German woods, a walk through the trees provides a canopy of peacefully rustling limbs, "as if / the woods had only ever known shade." But in that "as if", and the resonance of the ancient term for the souls of the dead, "shade", we find ourselves in a Black Forest of the underworld.

In what may be an homage to the great translation of *Gilgamesh* by her friend and mentor, David Ferry, Barber's brilliant version of a Mesopotamian story of the flood uses repetition and judiciously measured verse to evoke the ancient tragic scene in dignified earnest:

> As for us, how are we to live
> In a house of bereavement? How long?
>
> Let daylight return. Let the sun
> Light the crests of grasses, the crowns of weeds.
> Let the gods regret what they have done.

The title of the book, *The Sliding Boat our Bodies Made*, is taken from a poem that shimmers with erotic self-containment. These latent waves of tremulous longing are gorgeously manifest in the seascape cover painting by Barber's husband, the poet, translator, and prose writer Peter Brown.

In a tactful, elegant echo of Catullus, the poet's address to her own book ends with these breath-taking lines that will keep her poetry breathing long after the reader closes this discretely triumphant book:

> A wind rustling at the door
>
> of the cottage beyond the field
>   whose sleeper breathes the same
> evening. Lie down, my book:
>   lie down with the sleeper.

MARK WALSH

Book Review: *The Owl and The Nightingale: A New Verse Translation* by Simon Armitage
(Princeton University Press, 2022)

Late to the game (as usual), I recently started watching Showtime's drama series *Billions*. Four episodes in it became clear that the premise of the show boiled down to a high-stakes chess match between two masters who will only ever reach a draw; one gains the upper hand for a moment before Fate bestows a gift upon the other, and the stalemate is maintained.

I bring this up because, in many ways, this is the same structure of British Poet Laureate Simon Armitage's recent translation of the Middle English long poem *The Owl and The Nightingale* – a dialogue between two adversarial birds who debate, insult and maneuver each other to an eternal draw. All done for our delight, since the birds themselves are verbal craftswomen who educate and amuse the reader from start to stop.

The poet who composed *The Owl and The Nightingale* is a cause for serious detective work, and the subject of Armitage's informative introduction. The poem is hard to date or locate. Armitage's scholarship leads us to Master Nicholas of Guildford who resided in Portesham, Dorset; yet linguistic evidence makes a case for the poet hailing from Kent, or possibly Wessex, and writing sometime between the 12th and 13th Centuries. Given the considerable empathy this poem holds for the plight of women, one can infer that the poet was in fact a woman – a reasonable assertion, and a door that Armitage leaves open when reminding the reader that both birds are consistently referred to as she.

The fact that this long poem ends itself before a victor is crowned by an impartial judge (whose name I will not divulge, leaving that pleasure to the reader), enriches its charm. Both the nightingale and the owl are well-equipped to handle themselves – the nightingale nuanced and strategic, the owl intense and forceful – and do not give an inch to the other. The poem opens with insult, when the nightingale, in the practiced voice of a courtier, dresses down the owl, claiming the night hunter a "Freak" and filthy creature whose presence casts a shadow over the beautiful things.

> "Freak, why don't you disappear?
> It sickens me to see you here.
> Your ugly presence guarantees
> to throw my fliting out of key.
> In fact whenever you turn up
> my jaw locks & my heart won't pump.
> As for your tuneless yodeling
> it makes me want to spit, not sing."(lines 33-40)

The nightingale and her song are detuned by the presence of the owl, by the idea that a bird so noble must share the forest with one so base. It's an insult born out of class divisions. That's only the beginning. Like all well-crafted long poems, *The Owl and The Nightingale* is broad in scope, presenting topics as diverse as Christian stoicism, alchemy, Aristotle's ethics, astrology, scatology, iron smithy, marriage, war, the art of rhetoric, metaphysics, and more for the reader to uncover. Both birds espouse on topics according to their nature: the owl grimaces under uncomfortable truths; the nightingale attempts to rise to sympathetic ideals. The owl is of the earth, the nightingale of the spirit. Or if we look to Sir Philip Sydney's future thesis, the owl teaches, the nightingale delights.

Much of the poem is straight gamesmanship. The birds do not like each other, the nightingale viewing her opponent as perverse and morose, whereas the owl looks upon her opponent as superficial and weak. They trade insults, and speak the dozens to great effect, no better than the volley that transpires early in the poem. The nightingale begins:

> You smirk & simper when you hear
> Of men whose faces stream with tears.
> When wool gets tangled up with hair
> the weaver weeps & you don't care.
> That's where you stand – on sorrow's side –
> so when the snow lies deep & wide
> with every bird & beast forlorn,
> you drone your dirge from dusk to dawn. (425-432)

Up for the challenge, the owl strikes back, launching a defense that justifies how she provides aid to humankind, while reminding the nightingale she is not as pure as she thinks:

> & not one living things can wait
> to mount his mate & copulate,
> & frisky stallions in the stud
> would ride each filly if they could
> and you're the center of the throng
> with your debauched, licentious song…
> In fact, your song's worse than a sparrow's,
> grubbing through the stubbed furrows;
> once desire has run its course
> Your throat dries up & leave you hoarse. (493-98 / 505-8)

What's most interesting here is, although the birds are female, the insults they hurl at each other are decidedly male and too much occupied with sexual performance, or lack thereof.

The song of each bird, by which we take as their preferred style of poetry, reveals as much, if not more about these two contrasting figures than any bawdy insult. Both birds see their function as helping to manage human suffering ("Which man is best, do you believe, / the glad man or the man of grief?"). The nightingale sees her function as infusing her song with happy notes to help human beings know higher feelings,

> I manage more with just one song
> than you achieve the whole year long.
> For my great talent I am loved,
> for being brutish you are snubbed. (789-792)

Conversely, the owl deals in harsher realities, refusing to pretty anything up, believing an honest appraisal holds more value:

> My song of longing carries tones
> of lamentations in its notes,
> so man will know his crimes & grieve
> His misdemeanors; he'll believe
> the song I'm singing, urging him
> to own his guilt & mourn his sins. (869-874)

The nightingale understands escaping trouble, if only for a moment, gives us a respite and balance; the owl understands unvarnished truth, however ugly, gives us wisdom.

And yet, its core, I would argue, *The Owl and The Nightingale* is a poem about the perilous journey that women make through life. For all its comedy, for all its male posturing, the poem deals in hard truths that echo in the Wife of Bath's Prologue and Emilia's advice to Desdemona in Act V of *Othello*:

> The man who misbehaves that way
> can't fail to send his wife astray.
> Because of his abuse at home
> she'll seek out pleasures of her own;
> she'll cuckold him, of course she will,
> but don't say she's responsible. (1539-1544)

Women, the owl reminds us, have always struggled against overwhelming odds for personal and economic agency. But they also have their revenges.

There are many joys in reading Armitage's work, chief among them his attention to the technical side of the craft. His earlier translation of the Pearl Poet's *Sir Gawain & The Green Knight* demonstrated steady rhythmic control of alliterative verse. The same can be said for the ease of his lines here. Consider these six lines from the middle of the work:

> For love is proud & honorable
> Between a man & woman, though
> Not stolen love; that love is low,
> The sordid, grubby type. Well may
> The Holy Cross bring down its rage
> On those who act unnaturally –
> They must be made, And actually... (1378-1384)

Couplets (and ampersands!) are the stuff of this 13th Century, but like a good musician, Armitage locks in the metric pulse so confidently, he can stretch or extend rhymes at will.

Medievalists can drill down into this translation and debate the effectiveness of Armitage's updated version. This would make for good arguments in graduate courses, but for our purposes here, it's a wash. I spent some time comparing the facing pages of the Middle English original and Armitage's translation for a key into his decision-making process but doing so did not take away one laugh from the reading. If anything, I came away impressed with the muscular, consistent energy of Armitage's couplets. All 1794 lines are paced with perfect precision and when appropriate, comedic timing.

As with all beast fables, the reader is encouraged to interpret the allegory. *The Owl and The Nightingale* can be successfully read as a struggle between the classes, or between philosophies, maybe over the aesthetic purposes of poetry, an optimistic worldview vs. a pessimistic, and on and on. It is also too easy to read this poem as allegory for what ails our contemporary world with its anger and division but does remind us of what we have forgotten – to listen to opposing viewpoints. A poem is only as good as what the reader brings to it, but a poem that makes itself available to many readers at many levels is a poem to be taken seriously, no matter how much it makes us laugh.

ERIC HYETT

Book Review: *To Sleep with Bears* by Steve Nickman
(Word Poetry, 2022)

Steve Nickman's new book of poetry, *To Sleep With Bears* is an explosive exercise in narrative storytelling. The central event is a dramatic change in Nickman's marriage, when his wife of many years moves into Assisted Living. They sell their long-time family home, and Nickman moves into a condo by himself. This life change is so shocking that it goes off like an atomic bomb, and the resulting book of poetry is made of fallout: the poems are the individual shards of meaning a poet is able to capture as they fly around him. Those shards go back through Nickman's entire life.

This "explosionary" approach, with a lyrical examination of the wide-ranging psychic fallout from a central catastrophic event, apparently causes everyone who writes about "To Sleep With Bears" to devolve into lists. From the blurbs on the back of the book:

Wendy Drexler: "cats, moose, spider, parrot, and three squirrels; a peaceable lion in the poet's mind, who speaks in parable and longing"

Alexis Ivy: "formal, fable, persona, personal, antic"

Grey Held: "some lyrical, some narrative, both insightful and wise"

Lewis MacKinnon: "religious traditions, astronomy, psychiatry, childhood, child-parent relationships, nature, animal friendships, space, time, loss, expectations, desires, romantic love, couple-hood, parenting, child rearing, emotions and personification…"

There is a reason those authors are responding to this book with lists: because how else can you capture psychic fallout? Seriously, it takes chutzpah to put poems in a sequence that is non-chronological. It has to be done with intention, as Nickman does successfully in "To Sleep With Bears."

The book opens with three marriage poems that seem to be recent, and then comes a huge departure, a poem called "The Evangelist" set in North Carolina in 1962. We have young Steve Nickman as a person in the world, having a kind-of dialogue with a Black female evangelist, and if you were wondering what was the relevance to his marriage and contemporary times, the poem makes it very clear:

I hear her in Boston
on hot sunny mornings.

That's the thing about *To Sleep With Bears*, it isn't trying to be encyclopedic, or autobiographical at all. The "past" poetry isn't really past tense. It's a conveniently-remembered, ironic past tense that serves the book's present-day challenges. Similarly, poems in this book that seem to be exploring themes outside of love and marriage are not to be taken at face value. A favorite for me in that category is "In The Airport Lounge" where the speaker observes different groups of "withs" (i.e. people traveling together) using the language of birdwatching. As beautifully clever as this poem is, with its labeling of "sweetheart withs" and "athletic withs" and "tourist withs," it can't mask the fact that the speaker seems to be alone in observing all these "withs." And thus, back to the marriage.

In the following poem, "On The Boston-Paris Flight," the speaker is still traveling alone, he speaks with a young boy, summons an inner child, and again, right back to the marriage. Repeatedly, Nickman does the same thing: summon a necessary memory, deploy it beautifully, at an artistic angle, and get out of the way. The love poems that follow the airport poems are thus permanently colored by what we've just experienced: the loneliness from the airport poems bleeds through, even when Nickman and his wife are back together, so by the time we get to "In The Bedroom" and "Outage," we start to experience the deeply complex layered emotions of what it's like to be both lonely, and happily married, at the same time.

This psychic ikebana is extremely intentional. The entire book is highly intentional. Steve Nickman's bio refers to himself as "an almost-retired child psychiatrist" and the analytic framework behind his new book is so subtle, you could almost miss it. But isn't that the definition of good poetry: poetry that moves your reader? Who cares if we are being intentionally moved: so much the better!

Nickman is actually making a very rational argument, that the seeds of our present [dis]content are planted in our childhoods. "My Parents' Graves" sits directly opposite "Bonsai In A Malachite Ceramic," which renders me awestruck at how beautifully the power and strength of a book are enhanced by the scrambling of timeframes, juxtaposition of themes, and from the complex, multifaceted images being evoked across poems. With *To Sleep With Bears*, Nickman hasn't just written a good book, or a moving book, it is a legitimately heartbreaking book.

TOM DALEY

Book Review: *Now Calls Me Daughter* by Christine Jones (Nixes Mate Books, 2022)

"Everything these days / turns into a mother poem" writes the daughter/ poet of Christine Jones' *Now Calls Me Daughter*. "There's something / about the ambiguous loss / of her compelling me / to write her in." And indeed, the poems about a mother spiraling into dementia arrive, arrest, cajole, collude, conspire, one after a blessed another. Sonnets, free verse poems, list poems, even erasure poems, become the staircase we clamber up and down as the mother's disorientations compel our footsteps through the pages of this remarkable collection.

In the best poems of the book, the experience of dealing with her mother's illness provokes the daughter into the expression of something beyond the limits of complaint, disappointment, or concern. For a reader who seeks out the revelations potentially inherent in poems in which the language itself is the experience as much as the content, this is a great satisfaction. Jones allows the impact of the devastation to curb the rational, to unpin the subconscious, to broker new realties vested in language that, sometimes untamed and turbulent, serves to convey the odd disorientation of watching the mind of a parent devolve.

In "My Mother Asks Me to Write Her a Poem About the Sky," the daughter tabulates the effects of the displacements while she is in faraway Delhi: "I count each day in sugar crystals & fennel seeds. Underwater in a pool, the only place I can breathe—the world is smaller than it is." Sometimes, the poet/speaker is quite conscious of this effect, as when she admits, "Heavy mist forges my lines" and demands, "How to be understood?" ("What I Want to Say Driving Home After My Mother's Check-Up"). In the lines that follow, we are given a surrealism that penetrates into reality: "A rattled burst of air strews / a small opening in the windshield." Strews an opening? The contradiction of an opening being strewn into place distends the conscious mind, a perfect analogy for the sway of dementia over the victim and those who care for her.

This kind of response sometimes articulates the helplessness with which we watch the consciousness of our friends and relations dement. When the mother calls in the middle of the night, lost in vagaries, confused, stupefied by the illness, the daughter can only respond in a kind of kind: "I bring her closer, nearer / the sun's blaze & vanishing." Sometimes, the impress of all the trouble renders the poet a visionary, as in "the world / redeeming itself, revealing / a small hole in the screen." The revelations percolate up from the everyday—lines in the same poem that precede the redemptiveness include these:

> the raw slide of an oyster, sandflats'
> figure lines, loamy blooms, my strand of hair
> in the shower stall, a green-eyed girl
> in Delhi knocking on our dusty Subaru.   ["Not a Bird"]

A bittersweet sense of humor gurgles through this tragic assemblage. One gets the picture of orthodox Roman Catholics with an ironical appreciation of the sacred, as when the speaker suggests she might be perceived by her confused mother as the mother's sister who is a sister:

> Or I can be *ma tante* Reine, the nun
> who dwells in the convent by a pond
> where ducks feast on leftover ends
> of unholy host.

Though it was the leaf of the fig tree which hid the "shame" of Adam and Eve, the fig is also known for its capacity for fruition, as in "The fig tree putteth forth her green figs, and the vines with the tender grape give a good smell. Arise, my love, my fair one, and come away" in the Song of Songs. In *Now Calls Me Daughter*, the mother's carnality comes packaged in a tight wrapping: "Her mind / a fig tree / in a Victorian robe." The woman who observed birds with an almost erotic appreciativeness has acquired a touchiness about them. She is "Ill at ease / with the brush / of an osprey's wing."

The sonnet, albeit the unrhymed kind, seems to be enjoying a bit of a renascence in our day. But Jones employs rhyme to stylishly wry use in her sonnets, occasionally slant rhyming English with the mother's mother tongue, French, as in this witty pairing at the end of "Now in Autumn: Sonnet II":

And when the tree-frog hours come, she
briefly hears her name, *Maintenant.*

That the mother would think her name is *Maintenant* ("currently, now"; it literally means "to keep the same") provides a potent paradox in a situation in which sameness is dissolving along with the present.

The elegant design of the book by the Nixes Mate team of Michael McInnis and Annie Pluto is complemented by a series of erasure poems spaced throughout the book. A contorting black eraser comprised of representations of damaged neurons, dysfunctional microglia, and/ or reactive astrocytes stretches into entangled roots and starshapes. It pokes out wisdoms, aphorisms, and surprises as it surrounds and isolates words.

Other strategies in the book include a list poem using excerpts from the emails of an anxious father of the poet who is watching his wife loose herself from his grasp and a ghazal in the voice of the mother in which variations of phrases using "here" form the repetend that ends the second line of each couplet. We hear everything from "he's not here" to "not here" to "who's here," the varieties suggesting a mind turning on the axis of its own confusion.

Both the email list and the ghazal are written in straightforward conversational idiom, which is as it should be, I suppose, given that they are in the voice of the parents of the poet. But poetry as a transcript of somebody talking is problematic—rarely is the everyday talk (or the email text) of a character sufficiently charged at the level of expression to do one important part of the work of poetry, which is to uncover the potentialities of language beyond its literal meaning. This is a tension for me regarding some of the less memorable poems in the book—while the content is almost always compelling, the choice to use plainspoken language, contrasted with the more expertly crafted language of the better poems, disappoints.

That disappointment, however, does not in any way lessen my admiration for the achievement of these poems, which deliver an extraordinarily poignant narrative of an engagement, at both the conscious and unconscious levels, with one of the great tragedies of the human experience— the dissolution of the mind in the grips of dementia.

Book Review: **Wendy Drexler's Notes from the Column of Memory** (Terrapin Books, 2022)

After reading *Notes from the Column of Memory* I took inventory— I learned over a hundred new ways to understand wildlife. I now have witnessed a freeing process on how to interact with my childhood self. And this book has regenerated ways to examine the relationships I have with art, artifacts, landscapes, as well as my own body. Wendy Drexler speaks with the things unspoken to. Life is a dialogue staged in a poem. In this world she elevated her stories into what feels like myth, and it mesmerizes from cover to cover.

The poet opens by speaking as her childhood self, informed by herself today. She speaks internally. In the poem "Corral," she takes from the column of memory an experience and transforms it to the high art of a crafted poem. "I liked keeping his secret, / he'd trusted me with it. // I guarded it desperately. / It charged around inside me / like a herd of horses galloping // across a vast bare plain." The voice is the child holding the hand of the poet.

I love the way Drexler switches personal pronouns, i.e., he/she/them into the intimate *you*. She knows when to direct her tone. It is crushing when she speaks directly to her dead, to her body, to her reader, to her memory. When speaking to her body her tone sharpens into cutthroat that stings on the page. "Apology to My Ovaries" is a killer "...and my God, you were brave, // wore menstruation like a brightly flowered dress.", "...Forgive me // for evicting you in your dotage, not even / a hearing, your desk cleared in an hour." In "For My BRCA Gene Mutation", she also battles her body., This is the most devastating *you*, because it witnesses the poet speaking to herself in such a tough, brave way. The effect is that these poems don't give sympathy for the poet's health conditions but honor the poet's affirmations as she speaks directly and shamelessly to her conditions.

Throughout the five sections her relationships are at times told through details of utility, everyday appliances are how the poet learns things. Drexler accomplishes the acts of articulating what is found in the mundane, turning its language into poetic rhapsodies. Whether in a traffic jam, or detailing the world of cotton candy, there is insight found. My favorite example of this is in "Oranges", where the poet watches her mother juicing oranges. The mother squeezing oranges at first seems small until the poet tells us that squeezing oranges is how her mother endures, and gives us her child's response to that. Drexler chose this memory to share with the reader as a way demonstrate what the daughter took on once her mother died. "…that burning / bore through me, as if I had to // do something about it. Or for it." This poem passes on how to sustain the work of quenching thirsts.

By section three, we breathe into the rhythmic ode to the poet's dead mother that is uttered in a half crown of sonnets. This half-crown is in its own section as it is a departure from the familiar. Drexler is queen at transforming the foreign, or abstraction into the familial. The research, imagination, humanity is gorgeous. The poet has connected deeply to an artifact—"Burial of a Woman with the Blackened Shells of 86 Tortoises" and used it as a jumping off point to get into the personal yet patterned workings of a mother-daughter relationship. The tone, the telling on herself, "I forgot what she said (forgive me), I didn't listen.", as she interrogates memory in a profound way. In another poem, she recreates this similar structure of connecting an artifact— an ancient image of dancing bears in Bulgaria—to her inner relational life in the poem, "At Intermission" where we go beyond the moment into history, into so much more than what it is to bump into an ex-husband.

The poet not only makes the connections with artifacts, but, also succeeds in making connections with wildlife. How much is learned from animals in this book is astounding. I love "The Gannets at Cape St, Mary's, Newfoundland" when Drexler ends the poem, "I thought// all birds sang for beauty. / Not for beauty. I'll learn / to love them more for that." Her affection towards each animal she encounters throughout the collection is more than just witness, it is an intimate understanding of the creature—its nature and habits giving it the humanness that can be so relatable. Drexler gives testimony to a groundhog, countless turtles, bluebird, octopus, Barbra Streisand's dogs, racoon, carp, varieties of owls. She achieves in expressing their habitats, as she makes their facts into a thing of beauty.

Twice an actual note from *Notes from The Column of Memory* speaks, they are shaped as a column. These poems are the only ones that are centered aligned on the page. Every poem knows where it is on the page. This close attention to placement makes these two poems even richer with its messages. "…and you will see / your own face, fractured / but reclaimed,…" This moment is where the poet shows the potential and control the artist can have of her art at times. It almost feels like Drexler has held the muse and articulates what her whole book is working to do for her reader and for her own expression. *Notes from a Column of Memory* is a collection that reconsiders experiences, and the narrator of that experience is a poet holding her own hand. She holds every bird, parent, view, her own childhood making them all answerable to her presence, transcribing them onto the page. Her strength is her language. She carries all these voices; each voice is as attentive as her own.

VIAN BORCHERT is a noted award-winning expressionist artist, poet, and educator along with being a Notable Alumni from Corcoran George Washington University in DC. Borchert exhibits extensively within the US and internationally in major cities such as NYC, LA, London, along with a vast coverage in publications. Borchert had her artwork exhibited in prestigious places like Times Square – Broadway Plaza and Art Basel Miami Beach. Borchert is an educator teaching fine art classes to adults in the Washington DC area.

MARY BUCHINGER is the author of *Virology* (Lily Poetry Review Books, 2022), */klaʊdz/* (Lily Poetry Review Books, 2021), *einfühlung/in feeling* (Main Street Rag, 2018), and *Aerialist* (Gold Wake, 2015). She serves on the New England Poetry Club board and teaches at the Massachusetts College of Pharmacy and Health Sciences in Boston. Her work has appeared in *AGNI*, *Gargoyle*, *Interim*, *[PANK]*, *phoebe*, *Plume*, *Queen Mob's Teahouse*, and elsewhere. Website: www.MaryBuchinger.com.

BARBARA CANDIOTTI is an artist, photographer, and writer. *Star*Line* and *Eye to the Telescope* have published her poems. *Litro Magazine* has published an essay. Her digital art pieces have been accepted by *Phantom Kangaroo*, *Zoetic Press*, *Utopia Science Fiction Magazine*, *Invisible City*, *Star*Line* (Cover Art), *Evocations Review*, *Electric Spec* (Cover Art), *ParABnormal* (Cover Art), *Defunkt Magazine*, *Illumen Magazine*, *Cosmic Crime Magazine*, *Künd Writers*, and *The William and Mary Review*.

YUAN CHANGMING started the learn the English alphabet in Shanghai at age nineteen. With a Canadian PhD in English Yuan currently edits Poetry Pacific with Allen Yuan in Vancouver. Credits include 12 Pushcart nominations & 14 chapbooks (most recently *Homelanding*). Besides appearances in *Best of the Best Canadian Poetry* (2008-17), *BestNewPoemsOnline* & Poetry Daily, among others across 48 countries, Yuan served on the jury and was nominated for Canada's National Magazine Awards (poetry category).

J. DANIEL CLOUD has been a newspaper journalist (words, photos, and editing) for 25 years. He has a career-long fascination with walls, signs, and other "roadside distractions." Many of the buildings with graffiti or intentional signs he has photographed have since been demolished, so he is happy to have memorialized them. Cloud shoots with cameras dating from the 1920s to the 2010s, mostly on B&W film, which he develops and prints at his home in South Carolina.

DENNIS DALY lives in Salem Massachusetts. He graduated from Boston College and earned an M.A. in English Literature from Northeastern University. He has previously published nine books of poetry and poetic translations. Two other books have been accepted for publication: *Odd Man Out*—MatHat Press, and *Psalms Composed in Utter Darkness*—Dos Madres Press. Please visit his blog here: dennisfdaly.blogspot.com.

THOMAS DALEY leads writing workshops in the Boston area and online. Recipient of the Dana Award in Poetry, his poetry has appeared in *Harvard Review, Massachusetts Review, Fence, Denver Quarterly, Crazyhorse, Witness, Poetry Ireland Review, museum of americana,* and elsewhere. He is the author of two plays, *Every Broom and Bridget—Emily Dickinson and Her Irish Servants* and *In His Ecstasy—The Passion of Gerard Manley Hopkins,* which he performs as one-man shows. FutureCycle Press published *House You Cannot Reach—Poems in the Voice of My Mother and Other Poems,* in the summer of 2015. His latest chapbook is *Far Cry* published by Ethel Zine & Micropress, 2022.

ADAM DAY is the author of *Left-Handed Wolf* (LSU Press, 2020), and of *Model of a City in Civil War* (Sarabande Books), and the recipient of a Poetry Society of America Chapbook Fellowship for *Badger, Apocrypha,* and of a PEN Award.

GRADY DEROSA hails from Atlanta, GA. He writes to heal from lived experiences with grief, crime, addiction, and incarceration. After living in Brooklyn for many years, he's returned home to the southern forest. When he's not taking cold showers or walking in nature, you can find him meditating or watching seven-hour videos of trains in the countryside. He believes everybody loves something, even if it's just spicy potato chips.

CAT DIXON is the author of the forthcoming poetry collection What Happens in Nebraska (Stephen F. Austin University Press, 2022) along with five other collections and chapbooks. She is a poetry editor with *The Good Life Review* and an adjunct instructor at the University of Nebraska, Omaha. Find out more at her website: www.catdix.com.

SARA RIES DZIEKONSKI holds an MFA in poetry from Chatham University. Her first book, *Come In, We're Open,* won the 2009 Stevens Poetry Manuscript Competition. Her chapbooks include *Snow Angels on the Living Room Floor* (Finishing Line Press 2018) and *Marrying Maracuyá* (Main Street Rag 2021), which won the Cathy Smith Bowers Chapbook Competition. Her poems have appeared in *Slipstream, LABOR, Cathexis Northwest Press,* among others. She is the co-founder of Poetry Midwives Editing Services.

SUSAN EDISON's first full-length book, *Since the House Is Burning,* by MoonPath Press was published in 2022. Her chapbook, *The Body Lives Its Undoing,* was published in 2018. Poetry can be found in: *Bracken, Michigan Quarterly Review, The Naugatuck River Review, Scoundrel Time,; JAMA, SWWIM,* and elsewhere. She is a 2019 Hedgebrook alum and teaches at Richard Hugo House in Seattle.

KAREN FRIEDLAND is a nonprofit grant writer by day. Her poems have been published in *Constellations, Nixes Mate Review, Vox Populi,* and others. She was nominated for a Pushcart Prize, received the 59th Moon Prize from *Writing in a Women's Voice,* and had a poem hanging for a year in Boston's City Hall. Her books are *Places That Are Gone* and *Tales from the Teacup Palace.* She lives in West Roxbury, MA.

EVE GLASERGREEN is an emerging poet, prose writer, and artist from the Finger Lakes region of New York State. She grew up in New Jersey and she is a graduate of Cornell University and the University of New Hampshire MFA program. She lives in a Victorian house with her husband and four cats named after hobbits.

JENNY GRASSL's poems have appeared in *The Boston Review, Tupelo Quarterly, Laurel Review, Green Mountains Review, The Massachusetts Review, Ocean State Review, Lana Turner,* and other journals. Her work was published in a National Poetry Month feature of *Iowa Review, and Bennington Review* will publish her poem in an upcoming issue. Her manuscript *DEER WOMAN IN THE DINING ROOM* was selected as a runner-up for the Tupelo Press July open reading in 2021. She lives in Cambridge, Massachusetts.

PATRICIA HANAHOE-DOSCH's poems have been published in *The Paterson Literary Review, Rattle, The Atticus Review, Panoplyzine, Confrontation, Rust + Moth, American Literary Review, Apple Valley Review, The Red River Review, San Pedro River Review, Apt,* and *Thimble,* among others. Her books of poems, *The Wrack Line,* and *Fleeing Back,* can be found on Amazon.com or the FutureCycle Press website. Check out her website at https://pahanaho.wixsite.com/pathanahoedosch and Twitter @PHanahoeDosch.

MARY ANN HONAKER is the author of *Becoming Persephone* (Third Lung Press, 2019), and the chapbooks *It Will Happen Like This* (YesNo Press, 2015) and *Gwen and the Big Nothing* (The Orchard Street Press, 2020). Her poems have appeared in B*ear Review, JMWW, Juked, Little Patuxent Review, Rattle.com, Sweet Tree Review,* and elsewhere. Mary Ann holds an MFA in poetry from Lesley University. She currently lives in Beaver, West Virginia.

ERIC E. HYETT is the author of *Aporia* (Lily Poetry Review Books, 2022) A poet and literary translator from Boston, Eric and his co-translator, Spencer Thurlow, made the shortlists for the 2018 National Translation Award and the 2018 Lucien Stryk Asian Translation Prize for their translation of *Sonic Peace* by contemporary Japanese female poet Minashita Kiriu (Phoneme Media, 2017). Eric's poems, essays and translations are part of the ongoing dialogue in *Granta, The Georgia Review, Lily Poetry Review, The Hudson Review, World Literature Today* and *Modern Poetry in Translation..*

PAUL ILECHKO is a poet and songwriter. He lives with his partner in Lambertville, NJ. He is the author of several chapbooks. His work has appeared in a variety of journals, including *The Night Heron Barks, Louisiana Literature, Iron Horse Literary Review, Clackamas Literary Review,* and *Book of Matches.* His first album "Meeting Points" was released in 2021.

ALEXIS IVY is a 2018 recipient of the Massachusetts Cultural Council Fellowship in Poetry and the author of *Romance with Small-Time Crooks,* as well as *Taking the Homeless Census* which won the 2018 Saturnalia Editors Prize. She is an advocate for the homeless in her hometown, Boston and teaches in the PoemWorks community.

GEORGE KALOGERIS'S most recent book of poems is *Winthropos*, (Louisiana State University, 2021). He is also the author of *Guide to Greece* (LSU), a book of paired poems in translation, *Dialogos*, and poems based on the notebooks of Albert Camus, *Camus: Carnets*. His poems and translations have been anthologized in *Joining Music with Reason*, chosen by Christopher Ricks (Waywiser, 2010). He is the winner of the James Dickey Poetry Prize.

MARCIA KARP has poems and translations in *The Times Literary Supplement*; *Harvard Review*; *Agenda*; *Literary Imagination*; *The Guardian*; *Ploughshares*; *Partisan Review*; Penguin Books' *Catullus in English*, and *Petrarch in English*, *The Word Exchange: Anglo Saxon Poems in Translation* (Norton) and *Joining Music with Reason: 34 Poets American and British, Oxford 2004-2009* (Waywiser). Karp's *If by Song* (Lily Poetry Review Press, 2021) was a finalist for the New England Poetry Club's 2022 Motton Book Prize.

JEAN L. KREILING is the prize-winning author of three poetry collections: *Shared History* (2022), *Arts & Letters & Love* (2018), and *The Truth in Dissonance* (2014). She is Professor Emeritus of Music at Bridgewater State University and Associate Poetry Editor for *Able Muse: A Review of Poetry, Prose & Art*. She lives on the coast of Massachusetts.

ELIZABETH LOUDON is a fiction writer and poet published in the *Gettysburg Review, Denver Quarterly*, and *North American Review*, among others. Her debut novel, *A Stranger in Baghdad*, will be published in spring 2023 by Hoopoe, an imprint of the American University in Cairo. She has an MA in English from Cambridge University and an MFA from the University of Massachusetts Amherst. She's taught English at Smith and Williams Colleges and worked as a campaign strategist and writer for NGOs and Universities.

SHERRIE LOVLER is a painter and poet from Santa Rosa, California. She has been a calligrapher for decades and brings calligraphic marks and gestures to her paintings. Sherrie's award-winning book, *On Softer Ground: Paintings, Poems and Calligraphy*, features her painting and poetry. She teaches art classes both online and in person. Her work can be seen at: www.artandpoetry.com.

RADHA MARCUM's collection *Bloodline* received the 2018 New Mexico Book Award in Poetry and her poems appear widely in journals. A graduate of Bennington College and the University of Washington, Seattle, where she held the Klepser Fellowship in Poetry, Radha lives in Colorado where she writes the *Poet to Poet* newsletter (poettopoet.substack.com) and teaches at the Lighthouse Writers Workshop.

CHLOE YELENA MILLER's poetry collection, *Viable*, was published by Lily Poetry Review Books (2021) and her poetry chapbook, *Unrest*, was published by Finishing Line Press (2013). Miller is a recipient of a 2020 and 2022 DC Arts and Humanities Fellowship (Individuals) grant. She teaches writing at American University, University of Maryland Global Campus and Politics

& Prose Bookstore, as well as privately. She can be found at www.chloeyelena-miller.com / https://twitter.com/ChloeYMiller

CATHERINE COBB MOROCCO's poetry books include *Moon without Craters or Shadows* (Kelsay, 2014), *Dakota Fruit* (Turning Point, 2019) and a chapbook, *Prairie Canto* (2016). "Son's Story" won the Dana Foundation prize for poetry about the brain. Her books, *Visionary Middle Schools* (Teachers College Press 2006) and *Supported Literacy for Adolescents (Jossey-Bass 2008)*, focus on teaching for understanding. She taught at Harvard Graduate School of Education and Clark University and holds an Ed.D. from Harvard University,

JEFF OAKS' two books of poetry, *Little What* and *The Things*, were published by *Lily Poetry Review Books*. Oaks has published poems and prose in several literary magazines, most recently in *Field, Georgia Review, Missouri Review, Superstition Review*, and *Tupelo Quarterly*. His work has appeared in the anthologies *The Familiar Wild: on Dogs and Poetry, Brief Encounters: A Collection of Contemporary Nonfiction*, and *My Diva: 65 Gay Men on the Women Who Inspire Them*. He teaches writing at the University of Pittsburgh.

NORA PACE writes poetry, essays, and fiction. Her work has been published in *Rabid Oak, Emerge Literary Journal, The Maynard, Juniper, Cobra Milk*, and Barren Magazine. Her work explores the natural world, human relationships, duality, and wonder. She lives in Central Falls, Rhode Island with her partner and a cat named Lizard. She teaches high school English with a focus on social justice and is a board member of the Rhode Island Writing Project.

AMY PENCE authored two full-length poetry collections, including *Armor, Amour*, a hybrid book— *[It] Incandescent* (both Ninebark Press)—and two chapbooks. Her most recent is *Your Posthumous Dress: Remnants from the Alexander McQueen Collection* (dancing girl press, 2019). Poems are out or forthcoming in *Birmingham Poetry Review, Denver Quarterly*, and *Pleiades*. She's a full-time tutor and has taught poetry at Emory University and in other workshop settings.

ELIZABETH SYLVIA (she/her) lives with her family in Massachusetts, USA, where she teaches high school English and coaches debate. She is the winner of the 2021 3 Mile Harbor Book Prize and her first book *None but Witches* was published in 2022. Elizabeth's work is upcoming or has recently appeared in *The Southern Review, Feral, SWWIM, Thimble Literary Magazine*, and *Mom Egg Review*, among others. @e_sylviapoet

CAMMY THOMAS' newest collection, *Tremors* (Four Way Books), received Poetry Honors from the Massachusetts Book Awards in 2022. *Cathedral of Wish* received the Norma Farber First Book Award from the Poetry Society of America. A fellowship from the Ragdale Foundation helped her complete *Inscriptions*. In March 2022, *Far Past War*, an orchestral setting of her poems composed by her sister, Augusta Read Thomas, premiered at Washington DC's National Cathedral. She lives in Bolton, MA.

PETER URKOWITZ lives in Salem, Massachusetts where he works in a college library. He was drawn into the local poetry scene after the death of a poet friend when the community came together to remember and reflect. He stayed as a spectator and was soon led into writing his own work. He has been gratified by the warm and supportive response. He has published poems in *Meat for Tea: The Valley Review* and in *Oddball Magazine*. He is the author of *Fake Zodiac Signs: An Astro-Illogical Guidebook*

PAUL VIERA is retired and resides in western North Carolina. He is an avid art enthusiast having collected glass and metal sculptures, abstract and expressionist paintings, and found artistic expression in landscaping his yard. Earlier in life, Paul worked in human services and colleges in various locations including a time in the Republic of China - Taiwan. He recently began to experiment with designing wall art like the "Hendersonville Apple Tree" which pays homage to the local apple industry. This piece has been donated and is on display at the Hendersonville, NC Chamber of Commerce.

MARK WALSH is an English professor at Massasoit Community College in Brockton, MA. His recent publications include *Abandoned Mine*, *The Lily Poetry Review*, *Wilderness House Literary Review* and *The Beatnik Cowboy*.

CHAD WEEDEN'S work has appeared in *Jet Fuel Review*, *Asheville Poetry Review*, *Crosswinds Poetry Journal*, *Pedestal Magazine*, *great weather for MEDIA*, *Iodine Poetry Journal*, *Main Street Rag* & the *Kakalak*. He lives in Newport, Rhode Island.

CAL WENBY is an artist, poet, and photographer based in the UK. His work has been published in *Marsh Flower Gallery*, *Sonic Boom*, *Attic Zine*, *X-Peri*, *Queerly*, *Mad Swirl*, *Hidden Noise*, *Utsanga*, *Cafe Review*, *The Quarterly Journal of Art and Poetry*, *Interim*, and *Typo*.

BRIAN WHITMORE of Wigan, Greater Manchester, UK is a Calligraphy Artist practicing the wondrous art of painting speech to the eyes and Zen asemic/abstract mark making.

TERESA WILLIAMS lives in Seattle and Mazama, Washington. Her poems have appeared in *Psychological Perspectives*, *Third Wednesday*, *Lucia Journal*, *Vine Leaves Literary Journal*, *A Hundred Gourds*, *A Network for Grateful Living*, and elsewhere. When she isn't writing, she likes to wander near mountains and rivers with her beloved wolf-dog. She earned an MSW at the University of Washington and an MFA in poetry at Pacific University.

TOWANA WRIGHT was born in Mobile, AL and currently resides in Chelsea, MA. Although she moved from Alabama at a young age, the impact and the culture of the south would remain influential and serve as inspiration for her work and shape her as an artist. Towana pursued a lifelong dream and attained an MFA in Creative Writing. She graduated in 2015 and went on to participate in numerous prestigious workshops and residencies including traveling to Oxford University.

KENTON K. YEE has published poetry in *Plume, The Threepenny Review, Delta Poetry Review, and Pembroke Magazine*, among others. An Iowa Summer Poetry Workshop alumnus, theoretical physicist, and former Columbia University faculty member, Kenton writes from northern California.

MICHAEL T. YOUNG's third full-length collection *The Infinite Doctrine of Water*, was longlisted for the Julie Suk Award. He received a Fellowship from the New Jersey State Council on the Arts and the Jean Pedrick Chapbook Award. His poetry has been featured on *Verse Daily* and *The Writer's Almanac*. It has also appeared in numerous journals including *Banyan Review, Gargoyle Magazine, The Inflectionist Review, Talking River Review*, and *Valparaiso Poetry Review*.

www.ingramcontent.com/pod-product-compliance
Lightning Source LLC
Chambersburg PA
CBHW071157120626
46546CB00006B/2305